A Feast for Santa Barbara

Published by Gunpowder Press
Edited by David Starkey and Chryss Yost
PO Box 60035
Santa Barbara, CA 93160-0035

Cover photos: George Yatchisin and Le Petale Studio (Unsplash)

ISBN-13: 978-1-957062-30-3

Library of Congress Control Number: 2026904225

www.gunpowderpress.com

Gunpowder Press is part of Gunpowder Poetry, a 501(c)(3) nonprofit literary organization. *A Feast for Santa Barbara* is published as part of the Shoreline Voices Series which features area poets, ranging from new writers and younger students to awarded and recognized poets, with support from the Santa Barbara Poetry Fund under the auspices of the Santa Barbara Foundation.

A Feast for Santa Barbara

Poets Celebrating Food & Drink

Edited by

George Yatchisin

Gunpowder Press • Santa Barbara
2026

Contents

III. Labor

IV. MARKET

V. RITUAL

VI. Ingredients

As a writer who has long extoled the glories of Santa Barbara food and drink as both a journalist and a poet, I am thrilled by this collection of poems. I knew before becoming our city's Poet Laureate that I wanted to create an anthology like this one. Paul Willis (Santa Barbara Poet Laureate from 2011 to 2013) refers to the laureate's role as similar to that of a "secular chaplain." These are poems that say to you: *Take, and eat.*

There is a rich deliciousness in the variety and flavors in these poems, reflecting the diverse communities in our community.

I asked Krista Harris to write a brief foreword, knowing that her years as the publisher of *Edible Santa Barbara* would provide a grounding perspective for this collection. No one has spent more time thinking and writing about the restaurants, food, and agriculture in our community.

Thank you to the City of Santa Barbara, County Office of Arts & Culture, and the Santa Barbara Public Library for their ongoing support of the Poet Laureate program and other programs to encourage us all to savor literature and the stories surrounding us. Thanks to Gunpowder Press, co-edited by two past Santa Barbara Poets Laureate, David Starkey and Chryss Yost.

Thanks also to the Santa Barbara Trust for Historical Preservation, particularly its executive director Anne Petersen. The Trust's "Poetry Grows Here" workshop in the Presidio Neighborhood was the inspiration for many of the poems in this collection. Thank you as well to Cie Gumucio for being an inspiring teacher and liaison for the students whose poems appear here.

Finally, my appreciation to the poets who cooked up these delightful little morsels. As Julia Child, one of America's most recognized epicurians and a longtime Santa Barbara resident, would say, *Bon appetit!*

George Yatchisin
Santa Barbara Poet Laureate, 2025-2027

Before you turn the first few pages of *A Feast for Santa Barbara*, consider yourself warned: Santa Barbara seeps its way through poem after poem. From first libations to beloved locations, from the labor that sustains us to the markets that connect us, from the small pleasures to the rituals and ingredients that gather us in—this book reminds that a place can be told as well as tasted. Whether you devour the whole book in one sitting or sip and savor a single poem at a time, I suspect you'll feel nourished.

I count myself lucky that when I first arrived in Santa Barbara years ago, I landed in a poetry class at UC Santa Barbara taught by Robyn Bell. Sitting in a circle, listening to others read their work—and then writing and then reading my own—was a watershed moment. Around the same time, I was learning some curious things about Santa Barbara that involved tri-tip and Cold Springs Tavern; the farmers market and the Isla Vista Food Co-op; fresh seafood at the harbor and ordering spiny lobster at the end of Stearns Wharf.

The poetry and the food. It all just fueled my hunger for more. That's the thing about poetry—those delightful bite-sized courses of language. You read, you pause to think, and you savor. You step into someone else's world, their memory, their senses. Their poem might give you permission to dream of the past or sigh with longing or admit your hunger for connection.

These poems will send you away inspired—to eat and drink more of the local treasures, yes, but also to notice the histories and the hands behind them, and perhaps to write something yourself. I can think of no better tribute to Santa Barbara than to revel in the food and drink community that has evolved here. So, please join me in raising a glass, taking a sip, and turning the page.

—Krista Harris
Founding Publisher of *Edible Santa Barbara*

1.

Libations

Prescription

Physicians once prescribed the sun and salt air
of Santa Barbara to their patients, who traveled west
by train, once that final golden spike was driven in.

I myself would have prescribed the wine.
To be taken near the bougainvillea, I would have written,
or sipped beneath Italian stone pines.

To be savored among the sage and juniper of the foothills,
my barely discernible instructions would have read,
or on the beach in the company of the snowy plover.

To be tasted in the shade of an orange tree,
a pomegranate, a lemon, amidst the thrum of a hummingbird,
the silence of a monarch, the jasmine, jade and jacaranda.

Like these grapes, we too might adapt, might learn
to thrive under marginal conditions of stress.
In any case, what is thought to be the finest vintage

ceases to be, for an excess of attention corrupts appeal.
Push past the smoke and mirrors, the notes of plum and leather,
bay and olive leaf, beyond critique and commodity,

and you may arrive at the crossroads of work and weather,
of transformation and time. Here you will find art and science,
story and legend, geography and alchemy.

Here you will find the labor of many hands, knowledge
converging with leaf and clay, history class in a bottle.
For somehow, *in vino veritas*—there is truth in wine.

Pinot Noir from Santa Rita Hills

In the dark I did not know what I had in my hands,
a curved surface, smooth and fresh.
I turned on the light to find a glass half full.
The wine did not dissatisfy me.
I decided to get up,
survive all the insomnias of the world.
A wrong pronouncement becomes a blessing
and explores what abides within a Pinot from Santa Rita Hills.
On my tongue black cherry, mushroom, pencil.
At the bottom a tiny dancer,
dressed in crystal muslin,
spins non-stop on her axis.
Monolithic, with no hurry and no fractures.
She is not intimidated.
With tight core throws away what is useless,
who has disappointed her.

The Funk Zone

Sitting alone with my thoughts
canvas sails filter sunlight
above light bulbs strung
on an outdoor patio
surrounded by potted trees.

A train whistle blows loudly
murals lean across brick walls
salt air drifts inland from the harbor
and the hum of conversation
mixes with the cry of gulls.

I swirl the stem of my glass
look longingly into the red liquid
inhale its earthy aroma
taste its magical qualities.

It's a little light for my palate.

As if reading my thoughts,
a man beside me leans over, asks,
"How's the wine?"
I smile
"It's good. Though I thought it would be more full-bodied
given the name Blood Moon."

He smiles back
simply says, "Cheers,"
pays his bill and leaves.

I sit back in the white metal chair
shuffling decomposed granite under my feet
observing people lose themselves
in each other's company
savoring precious pressed grapes.

I drink to the sweet salt air
to the city by the sea
to this charming neighborhood winery
where thoughts and people mingle.

For a moment
in the Funk Zone
we all breathe together.

Wine Country

In a drift of clouds we raise
our glasses to the Chardonnay sky—
praise its turn toward Rosé.
Day slips from our grasp
along with varietal complaints.
Another sip. Sky goes Cabernet,
more Zinfandel as we link arms

around each others' waists
and refrain from speaking the cliché
about age deepening with time,
but it's there. A little tipsy
under wraps, like Syrah
someone laughs. We toast *Hurray*

eyes focused on the blurred horizon
watching sun melt then crash
behind the hills and suddenly
it's all Pinot Noir. One
with an old ritual, we bow
in silhouette, red spreading
like a river in the blend.
Vina, vini, vitae—

"Here in the Electric Dusk"

After winter rains
The hills
Are velvety beasts
We pretend
We have nothing
To worry about
Except for the usual
Minuet of dying
Scraping the corners
We drink the dark
Ardor of Sangiovese
As if we were in Italy
Haze of ancient coastal
Walls holding the highway
We thread in silver
Our headless forms
Unafraid of breaking
Open. We are really
Not so far away
In this valley sighing
Green at last it has
Stopped raining the sky
Gets soft when that happens
I feel it in my eyes
Where I swallow
So much I have nothing
To say that is wise
I just sit beside
A persimmon tree
With my loves
Drinking what was
Poured for me
Until the end
Of the day lifted

Her sheet of fire
Cutouts of dimming
Oaks and the mountains
The mountains the
Mountains and us
Calling ourselves
Home.

When in the Zone

From the Rising Place to State, a state of

anticipation, of delight, of adventure, to the Shuttle,

trundling with stoic little-engine-that-could importance.

To the end, to the ocean, then on to the Zone. First stop, a

welcoming winery with aromas of barrels, grapes, day drinkers.

With friends, a man wearing a white tank top raises his glass.

Any other city, he'd be in a sports bar, gripping a beer stein.

His friends, loud, laughing, lingering, answer his toast.

Here we celebrate with sophistication.

We hold the

Stem

Squint

Swirl

Sip

Swish

Sigh.

Eyebrows raised, we smile. On to the next stop,

the next cozy sunlit room, on to new tastes and toasts.

Ice Breaker

when bringing strangers together
with any possibility
of fruitful engagement
consider the fruit of the vine
whether red or white
dry or sweet
Pinot or even Merlot
the blood between your guests
will flow, like the tubes in a lab
pumping youthful elixir from
beaker to beaker
words begin to slip, mingle, perhaps
even enchant with mystery and humor
a little broken ice and we are chipper
less solemn, less bound to the small chapter
in our dark corners of curling pages on
this twirling, dizzying planet, a little wine
raised in good spirits, won't increase the dizzy
but may unify the spin

The Wine Man at the Grocery Outlet

Knows his Bordeaux
In this modest place in a parking lot
On De La Vina which is all torn up because of
Stuff they're doing to protect the creek.
There's people here struggling to pay
For groceries and here I am with the
14-dollar Beaune wine that usually goes for 50
I feel embarrassed
But the wine man doesn't think less
Of me for wanting something so fancy
In this floridly fluorescent place.
You get to want and get really good raspberries here
And excellent meats
You get to want and get those things at a good price
And the wine man nodding at my
Choice reminds me that is ok to
Want good things to eat and drink
In this land
Of plenty—
There really
Is enough
Good food for everyone—
We just need the will to
Provide it.

Wine

> *I like to drink wine more than I used to—*
> *anyway, I'm drinking more . . .*
> —Don Corleone

All day, the twine crisscrossing my heart—
the way they used to tie up parcels for the post—
tightens by degrees . . . but at last, in my lawn chair,
in the early evening shade of the stone pine,
a first glass of Pinot Noir, bruise dark, big with fruit,
loosens the knot and lets me breathe out into the sky,
far enough away from the world to love the honeysuckle
swimming up the stem of the air, the pink foxgloves
aligned like tiny Venetian cups.
                    Each sip calms me
like wind quitting over the bay, like the light trickling
down plum leaves. . . . I look west toward Santa Cruz
where I can almost feel the clouds stationed above
the island going red against the sun, sweet as
a local Sangiovese, and lifting lightly from my chest.

Mixers Speak Up

We have long bubbled quietly below the bar,
confined to plastic containers and flip top cans,
or squirted like wet bullets from a soda gun.

We hereby declare war on the caste system of cocktails,
weary of being supporting actors, low on the list
of credits. We want top billing!

Why Rum and Coke, not Coke and Rum?
Why all the booze-y names? *The Good Lion*
has its title right. Literary, like Hemingway—Yes!

Why Tequila Sunrise instead of *The Sun Also Rises*?
Why a Shirley Temple instead of a *Lolita*?
Please. We are not illiterate liquids!

Mixers happen to read between closing time
and next day's happy hour. We are highly educated
libations. Not to mention—Splashy.

Hard liquor lives under strict jigger laws,
in a 1.5-ounce prison, while we free-pour with a twist.
Like a Zen sand painting,

we are Buddhist. Think non-attachment!
A drink is ephemeral. Truly a *Spirit in the Air*.
It is mixed. Admired. Drunk. Gone.

So, we propose a toast. May all drinks be created equal.
May every beverage effervesce as one—an intoxicating
constellation of stars served in a cut-glass sky.

II.

LOCATION

Weekday at Brophy's

Sitting on a stool with a front-row view,
on a Wednesday afternoon
day moving so slow
I forgot it ever began.

Bloody Marys got some heat,
Oysters slide down like binge-watching Netflix—
Are you still watching?

The breeze eases the knots in my shoulders
old sea dogs talk like their lungs are rusted,
laughing at nothing,
their voices rise and fall
like the tide is part of the joke.

Gulls scream like the junkies on State
spinning circles 'round sails in the harbor.

While men in wool caps
hauling lines and crab traps
drag the sea behind them.

And those legacy kids
swaddled in their parents' cash,
float past on paddleboards and kayaks—
lit by a sun someone else hung in the sky.
Too pampered to touch reality,
too busy curating a life online
to enjoy their privilege.

Pour me another one, Mason, I'm under a spell—
something might just finally break my way for once.
Like finding a pearl
in an oyster,
or seeing a mermaid,
or another excuse
to stay longer.

Red Booth Restaurant

So much depends upon a red booth restaurant
when your destination is the past. You remember
the satiny slide across leatherette, the sociability
of a corner table. If you were born after World War II,
Harry's giant menu offers the same food
you grew up with and go on eating. Meat Loaf.
Cobb Salad. Prime Rib on birthdays. Photos fill
every wall with booth-to-ceiling celebrity shots—
Reagan on a horse, Fiesta Queens, photos of old
Santa Barbara, a huge moose head above
the swinging door to the kitchen. The noise level
accelerates as ladies and gents down round after
round of hefty cocktails. By dessert, quiet women
get loud. Strident men quiet down.

Locked down in Covid, we relied on Harry's to fill
an emptiness worse than hunger. Masked, I tried
to put a smile in my eyes receiving our order
from the masked cashier—burgers, patty melts
with fries, small packets of catsup and mayo I tore open
with my teeth. I wasn't looking for deep conversation,
but to be with another ally against intangible dread.
This is just to say, you can still get anything
you want at Harry's restaurant.

The Santa Barbara Restaurant Scene

Inspired cuisine! Oceanfront views!
Featured in the local news,
A tradition since '39
The atmosphere is just divine

California-French cuisine
Creates a picture-perfect scene
Fare enhanced by fancy wines
"C'est bon!" say patrons here, who dine

Hearty American fare,
Try the special, if you dare,
Taste our sea urchin spaghetti
No long wait; we're at the ready

Historic downtown café
Appetizers on a tray
Stiff cocktails and vibrant bar
Draws a crowd from near and far

What happened to the State Street vibe?
It's hard to say; I can't decide
Funk Zone beckons us to come
'Cuz tasting wine is so much fun

French cuisine with coastal twist
"Bon Appétit!" ... you get the gist
Bistro only two doors down
Best in the entire town

Oaxacan-inspired Mexican
Views beyond comparison!
String lights create a magic glow
Best vibe on the patio

Stroll the harbor or breakwater
Clam chowder? French fries, a burger?
Dining options, ocean vistas,
Staff includes some fine baristas

Irish pub experience?
Only the best ingredients!
Music, drinks and lots of talk
It's so close that we can walk

Window seat, waterfront views
Enjoy a drink, no waiting queues
We recommend signature quiches
Guests enjoy our shellfish dishes

Santa Barbara wine is best
(We carry others, I confess)
Organic and digestible
A winner of the Festival

Waiting Tables at the El Encanto Inn in the Eighties

Each morning under the wisteria blossoms
I walk past the table of Floating Islands,
the dessert tray, and the cheese plate,
to where the maître d' sits, white bib
tucked into his collar like a king
eating his daily omelet. "Good morning
Chou Chou," he says as we arrive
to that vast blue and white painting
called the Santa Barbara Riviera.
This view is what the people come for.
That and a taste of the good life.
Celebrities, honeymooners, and troikas of ladies.

Once Robin Leach lifted a glass
here to his fellow elites, while I served
a salad and cameras rolled.
I waited on Joan Rivers, small and quiet
in her big sunglasses. Waiters fought daily
over who would bring a hamburger
to Stevie Nicks in her bungalow.

It was the days of Nouvelle Cuisine.
Portions resembled tiny ballerinas
dancing in a drizzle of sauce, a feather of green.
The more exotic the entree, the better.
Hippopotamus tongue was once a special.
Conger Eel another. The walk-in refrigerator—
my National Geographic hell.

I've become an expert at
the sleight of hand slipping corks
from their necks, the pop of champagne
into my waiting napkin.

In the kitchen, warm bread.
Wait staff bent over
some precious untouched leftover
for a taste of what we couldn't afford.

Filet of Sole

We've landed a table for two.
It's Valentine's Day *Chez Citronelle*,
overlooking the Santa Barbara harbor.

The waiter's tie
is screened
with Klimt's *Kiss*.

A trio of courses appears
in slow succession:
lobster bisque,
filet of sole,
chocolate soufflé.

Two tables over, a dark-haired man—
mmm—
takes off his shoes,

so do I, too—

as the waiter hands me a long-
stemmed rose
and my husband
                the bill.

Jeannine's

One State Street

The end of every month
finds me a little low
especially in August
when the moon is old

and shrinks to nothing.
We always meet for lunch
at the street end of the wharf
under the shade of faded umbrellas.

We sip mint muddled lemonades
but have no appetite for prettily
dressed greens with carrot curlicues
and cheery half tomatoes.

It's harder now the stairs,
I'm moving there, far from here...
Last call. Last bites.
Is it really over?

Summer drowned
by the barely warmed ocean.
Six am dark now
threatening, Autumn.

I Fell in Love at Brophy Bros.

Sure, with the boy sitting across from me,
but really, truly, deeply
with the clams placed before me—
The tangy broth,
the tender morsels,
the rich butter,
but more than that,
the moonlight on the water
and the lamplight on the dock
that we had just danced under.
The night was young
the mood was right,
and the clams were perfect.

Alas, summer swept in,
boiling and breaking that boy and I apart.
And so I needed something new,
fresh clams for a fresh start.
I had not far to go:
to the Fish Market just down the way.
A recipe for stuffed clams
to fill my empty heart,
I ate them doused in wine
with the crunch of bacon bits.
Tipsy on the summer sun,
I felt whole again.

I've been back since
to visit Brophy Bros.
I'll admit the moon didn't seem quite as bright.
But the same swirling sea seemed to say
that wasn't true,
because the clams, those perfect briny bites,
they were still just right.

The Plums of Lucinda Lane

for Nicole

Those summers moved slower than light—
spilling across our childhood's cracked patios,
afternoons pooling warm around our ankles.

All we needed was a low wall to sit on
& a portable radio tuned to *The Mighty 690*—
the soft ache of waiting for the world to begin
born in the lyrics of 80s pop songs. We were 10.

Nicole lived in the brown, two-story house
with the plum tree out front—its scarred branches
sprawling over the walkway. Each day the fruit hung
heavier, swollen—some splitting from their obscene
ripeness—the color of bike-accident bruises.

The first bite surprised us, flesh so warm it felt like
we were eating summer itself. We didn't talk much,
just passed plums between us—a stillness made of juice-
stained fingers, sunburnt legs stuck to hot concrete,
& the faint tick tick tick of a sprinkler somewhere.

Some afternoons, plums dropped on their own, staining
the sidewalk with a dull thud. We never ate those.

I didn't think about any of this back then.
Now, driving through San Roque in late summer,
I suddenly find myself on Lucinda Lane—memory
taking the wheel.

The street is narrower than I remember, houses
closer together. Nicole's house is still there, but the tree
is gone—cut down, vanished quietly like most things
that grow in one place for too long.

The curbs are crowded with cars, their windshields
catching the same sun that once poured over our knees
while we sat in the simple grace of doing nothing.

That's the thing about childhood: it gives you just
enough to spend the rest of your life missing it.

Artichoke

Thank you, Ca Dario

Every birthday and anniversary
they would eat out and order stuffed artichokes.
She enters a later decade and he orders them
again with fresh basil, tomatoes, extra garlic,
a bottle of Syrah.
Their words arch over the basket of bread.
Worries line up like fork and spoon alongside
the salt and pepper in their little towers:
her frozen shoulder, his heart arrhythmia,
their son's tuition, the growing fire.
They offer a cadence to their talk.
There are more dead than ever,
extreme weather is a fact.

They pull off leaves one by one, scrape on sweet
meat with teeth, savor the stuffing.
Food tastes as good as ever.
Smoke rises over the mountain of their town,
destruction in the air. *Do we eat what is burned*
one of them ponders. *Do we flavor it with garlic*
and hot peppercorns? What is given,
what is lost—part of the conversation.

They return again to the grace of flowers on the table,
appetizers guaranteed, bountiful pastas, tiramisu,
a celebratory song, in an overpriced overdressed city
they hang onto in the lives they have chosen, been given.
Happy birthday he says raising another glass—
the heart of chokes eaten. The prize worth the work.
Leaning forward, they kiss, one more year alive
and hungry, among the ruin and bloom of the world.

At a Cafe with a Four-Letter Name

Three cups, cradled
   close as teeth
and washed out white
   foaming at the lips,
Resting on his fingertips
   up past the crux of his wrist.
Delivered, carefully
   to the curve of the table,
Warm ceramic on cold glass
   biting the silence away—
Cappuccinos, for here?

Morning Coffee

"Greg!"
The barista calls out my name
With a rising voice
As though asking,
"Are you still here?"

I carry my cappuccino,
Full to the brim,
Overflowing even,
Its milky foam swirls undisturbed,
Back to my table
As carefully
As a newborn baby

The travel, the line, the wait, the anticipation
Melt away
Soon to be replaced by
The simple act
Of savoring

Savory

7:05 am. Place order.
Preheat oven. 400 degrees.
Brisk 4-block walk. Pick up. Return.
Set kitchen timer 7 minutes.
Plate ready.
I wait. Remember . . .

> *My first morning in Santa Barbara.*
> *Ignore the moving boxes, leave, explore.*
> *I ask two women hurrying to the film festival,*
> *"A neighborhood bakery?" They point 'that way'.*
> *I'm launched.*
>> *A block to go, my mind travels*
>> *330 miles to what I left behind—*
>> *friends, favorite food, places.*
>> *Daily walks to the bakery*
>> *through Dolores Park, 18th to Guerrero,*
>> *join a line of locals, tourists,*
>> *sometimes Parisians.*
>> *Nine years "there," one day "here."*
> *I've arrived.*
> *Inside, buttery baking smells.*
> *The pastry case—a palace of pleasure.*
> *Watched over by puffed up croissants,*
> *mahogany blistered or snowy with almonds.*
> *Sturdy cinnamon rolls guard delicate,*
> *jewel-toned confections, glistening*
> *cherry and blackberry tarts.*
> *Sweet artistry.*
> *I yearn for savory.*

The timer chirps.
Careful transfer, oven to plate.
My fork glides through a smooth alchemy—

eggs, cream, flecks of ham, nutmeg—
to a tender crust.

Thank you,
Chef Renaud Gonthier.
This quiche,
the taste of home.

Breakfast at Mulligan's

First bite and I didn't expect the rush of tears. Wasn't it yesteryear's meme: Crying While Eating? All those people videoing themselves eating while crying crocodile tears. Whenever I return from a trip away from Santa Barbara, I always order a Santa Barbara omelet from Mulligan's and the waitress who shares my name. Melinda rarely hands me a menu, knows how I will order a Santa Barbara omelet, but today I surprise her, ask for chorizo. I then surprise myself. Cry into my breakfast. The day is December 5, my mother's birthday. She would have been 76 this year. I remember the last time she cooked chorizo with eggs. We were at her friend's house where we always felt at home. Mom, ever the experimenter, found mushrooms, cilantro and cheddar cheese. I look up from my plate, see a woodpecker, its red capped head easy to spot as it flits from palm to palm. Too many memories in the cold swirl of red eggs on my plate. Without asking any questions Melinda takes my plate, returns with a Santa Barbara omelet with green sauce, black beans and an English muffin. Next time, I will order the usual.

Lilac Pâtisserie

I almost feel normal again as I gaze at the frosted perfections
displayed jewel-like behind the glass. Gawking at the full menu,

my mind spins with possibilities—I can choose anything;
can easily imagine eating here for weeks, never once

duplicating a dish. Suddenly, all the cakes
that became cardboard in my mouth,

all the sandwiches that crumbled between my fingers,
the eggs benedict and key lime pies, filled with gluten,

and declined at numerous gatherings, formal dinners,
casual meetups—they all fade like ancient Polaroids.

I   can choose   anything.

Belgian waffles and sugar-dusted
fruit; ripe red strawberries, buried

in sweet white frosting, protecting
layers of delicate yellow sponge;

pastries—I spent years pretending
were only figments of a starving imagination;

cute lemon-blueberry and key-lime tarts;
cheesecakes; layer cakes—frosted

chocolate with fruit or white with perfect
pink and yellow flowers.

Lilac Pâtisserie: one hundred percent
gluten-free treasure. My safe oasis,

where I can remember
and be free.

In The Heart of Downtown Western Girl Eats Her Lunch

I'd always liked the order and rhythm that a cafeteria
brought to the middle of the day
in elementary school and later in high school
as you moved along the line with your tray
food servers on one side of the glass, students on the other

you'd think the cozy old cafeteria on State Street
near so many of my temporary job assignments
would be a beacon of comfort and familiarity

but the beautiful old foliage around the entrance to
The Copper Coffee Pot did not comfort but intimidate
the people inside seemed so sure of themselves and their choices
some even looked like they'd been there since the 1927 opening
plenty of time to become acquainted

when all I felt was unsure like a panic-stricken kid
they didn't call the employment agency Western Girl for nothing
I wanted to walk up the block to the Woolworth's lunch counter
order a chicken salad sandwich and a Coke, be done with it

but I decided to stick it out till I couldn't take it any more
just pointed to the same dish the lady in front of me ordered
took my tray to a table, there that wasn't so hard
I felt proud of myself being so adult in my new town
ready to enjoy my nice hot lunch in my favorite new cafeteria

but you know, I haven't eaten liver and onions since

Fall-ing into Santa Barbara

Autumn delights its way into Santa Barbara once again.
Fog-shrouded downtown streets beckon the early riser
To don a sweater and follow the enticing aromas
From Handlebar, Dune, and Cajé coffee roasters,
Where pumpkin-spice lattes and buttery croissants await.
Those looking for a full breakfast
Make their way to Goodland Waffles and Melts on State Street,
Or head to The Boathouse at Hendry's Beach,
Where you can walk off your crab cakes and poached eggs
With a stroll on the sand.

The marine layer lingers through lunchtime,
And the smoky heat of tacos de rajas
Warms the heart and soul at La Super-Rica Taqueria.
Never fear—the wait in line along the sidewalk is always worth it.
Office workers pressed for time phone in their orders
For pastrami, corned beef, and Philly steaks at Norton's Deli on Figueroa.

The days grow shorter, and the evening breeze picks up
As the streetlights come on in the gathering mist.
The chilly night calls for some warm comfort.
Perhaps some Bangkok street noodles from Empty Bowl,
Or maybe a coconut corn chowder
At the Organic Soup Kitchen on Haley.

It's autumn in Santa Barbara—
Can't you just taste it?

Renaud's Patisserie

murky shadow on a page
and a crumpling wrapper
teeth slowly sinking
into a crispy baguette
and polite laughter
bird song, solitary
above the cafe
    a ding of the register
    the rumble of the till
        coins sloshing and abruptly stopping
           and a dry cough
        escaped from a cavern
   in my chest
        steaming milk and the whirl of metal
    like wind being birthed from a rapid
a heavy bell resonates from the south
        sounding the hour
           again
      sounding the hour
    jazz trumpet in triumph
on the radio and mingled with
    a mangled scratchy voice memo
     garbage truck sighs as it stops
    on the street behind me
   a second bird has joined the chorus
continuing to whistle and chirp hello
to the morning sun
    as a child sings a rhyme
      the shadow is being pushed off
  to the left of my parchment
    by the lazily unfurling sun
       a flutter of wings
    cheap heels striking concrete in rhythm
    like hooves on cobblestone

a sniffle and ceramic plates clattering
a language all its own
     as a black crow tolls the hour
          the roar of ocean waves
        a moving trash bin
            being pushed across asphalt
        on hard plastic wheels
lovers in front beaming and gaily chatting
the clinking of cutlery on a tin table
being jostled for position
     as the shadow loses its battle
        sunlight has prevailed

Breakfast the Most Important Meal of the Day

I met David at the Shoreline Café, we were there to discuss my manuscript over breakfast and drinks. I was hungry so I had the country scramble, bacon, potatoes, spinach, mushrooms, onions, cheddar-jack and toast with Scotch on the rocks. David had the two egg breakfast with bacon and a light bodied white wine. One thing I've learned, with Scotch on the rocks you can't go wrong. While we ate we discussed the manuscript for *First Sight*, I was to join Glenna and Jackson at Mille Grazie Press.

The food and drinks were worth the wind that morning on the beach, Ledbetter Beach, with the tables and chairs on the sand. After all "there is something big as the ocean inside you."

Ode to The Good Lion

After Ernest Hemingway's The Good Lion, *a children's story*

Because I like a pretty bar that serves cocktails named "Strange Beasts," I raise my glass to The Good Lion. And again to Ernest Hemingway, who made the lion good—who gave him golden wings to match his mane, and a distaste for zebras, wildebeests and antelope. The Good Lion preferred to eat tagliatelle and drink Negronis.

Of course in our world there is no good without bad, and the bad lions made fun of the Good Lion's wings and called him a son of a griffon. It is the same old story—the plain-nosed reindeers shunning Rudolph. These bad lions were so bad they were wicked. Besides their usual prey they ate people. They ate Swahilis, Umbulus and Wandorobos. The most prized delicacy of all—Portly Princes, rare and delicious.

One day the wickedest lioness wanted to taste the Good Lion's wings, but he escaped her claws caked with bloody Portly Prince and rose into the air—a golden apparition of goodness. The bad lions roared and the wind from his wings blew them to the ground.

The Good Lion left the savage beasts of Africa and flew home to Venice to visit his ancient, bronze father, still guarding the Basilica in St Marks Piazza with undying devotion. Hungry and thirsty from his journey he stopped in Harry's Bar. "A Negroni, Signor Barone?" asked Mr. Cipriani. "No," answered the Good Lion, surprising even himself, for Africa had changed him. "I'll have a dry martini made with Gordon's Gin. And do you happen to have any Portly Prince sandwiches?"

Once more I raise my glass to the Good Lion, and to Ernest Hemingway, who made the lion good and just a little bit bad.

Fear and Loathing at Elsie's Tavern

10:00pm

Smoking cigarettes
at the dive bar where
    my parents met: strange
art hangs from the walls
    & I wish to be home.

10:30pm

Washed my hands
at the restroom sink—
    cupped warm water
in my palms. Rinsed,
    almost genuflecting

to someone's phone
number, etched into
    the mirror. When I call,
I'll know you by the sound
    of your breath.

11:00pm

Dumping hot sauce
in my bowl of noodles.
    The barman sneezes:
a Poptart springs into
    action, snaps

into place. Nobody flinches
when the 8 ball shatters
    the window. Nobody
flinches, shooting 8 balls
    in the slender alley

across the street.
My 12th grade math
    teacher lurks a table
full of 21's. Some things, surely,
    just don't add up...

11:30pm

    like how someone,
somehow, is working
    on their thesis
in the corner booth.
    Frisky lovers scratch

    away at each other
beneath a flaking
    portrait of the
crucified Christ. Tenderly,
    the joint is ashed

    into a cold glass of
Miller Lite. Now listen,
    I know I'll be the first
one to tell you, the point
    of a pool cue

    is also called the tip.
At 12 o'clock, the crazies
    will start to filter in.
The radio goes all Mazzy Star—
    sneaking away

12:00am

    from this cozy bar,
I won't notice the body in the
    dark—or if, tonight,
the eucalyptus leaves are
    filled with shadows

or their quiet flitting.
Let's not even mention
    the moon; the little
family of raccoons forming
    a train along the courthouse

    lawn. But the old man
in the bushes. Dregs in his
    Styrofoam cup. Lying down
at the edge of the silent park,
    curling up, as if asleep.

Vintage Vinyl Love and the Cheese Shop

I enter the little haven of delights
on Santa Barbara Street after a visit

to Warbler Records with *The Kinks
Part 1– Lola Versus the Powerman*

tucked under my arm. Head full of
music to counter the dark of recent

days, I indulge, peruse charcuterie,
wines and cheeses that could satisfy

the most down-hearted of hearts.
A sweet monger steers me from one

flavor to the next with taste after
taste after taste tests until we reach

Sophia which flickers on my tongue.
Oh, *Sophia*, so bright and smooth

yet tangy, lifts me from my blue-funk.
She's complex, made of goat's milk

gifted enough to make most anyone
bleat or sign up for yoga with hoof

treks along their spine. At home with
with *Sophia*, a bottle of Bordeaux Blanc,

I spin the song *Apeman* over and over
and over again *happy in my apeman world.*

III.

Labor

The Hands that Mend

Seeds are delicately planted in a cool bed of soil
Once tucked, they are left to rest and grow
Weeks, months, years
We patiently wait

After the dew has dried and the sun begins to rise
Calloused hands carefully harvest the awaited supply
Ensuring quality and vigor

Transported to the hands of a cook
The chef chops, slices, kneads, and prepares through a blaze of fire
Sprinkling spices, warmth, and love
Diligently creating a work of art inspired by nature
Ensuring nutrients and satisfaction

The surrounding atmosphere radiates a sense of happiness
You can hear servers gradually pouring puckering wine
The clinking of glasses
Soft jazz echoing
Laughter
Ensuring connection and support

As the noise slowly diminishes throughout the crisp evening
Metal and sprays of water can finally be heard
Plates wiped clean are placed in the hands of a dishwasher
Humidity and grease consistently surge
Spending hours in the dish pit
Ensuring sanitation and supply

Hands must join to create this unifying cycle
All possess a different purpose, but all are essential
We are the hands that bring comfort and healing
The hands that provide gentle care and strength
The hands that create harmony

We are the hands that mend

Coffee for the Calloused

I open my doors with the morning sun,
Steam from the pot, day's work begun.
Boots hit the floor with a rhythm and beat,
Stories and sawdust dragged in on their feet.

They come in with grit, with grease on their hands,
With backs that have bent for ungrateful lands.
But here there's a pause, a soft kind of grace,
A hot cup, a smile, a welcoming place.

No fancy pretenses, no polished routine,
Just coffee that's strong and a counter that's clean.
I see them, I know them, I honor their name—
The ones who show up through struggle and strain.

They fix the roads and raise the walls,
Drive the trucks and answer calls.
And while the world may rush right past,
I slow it down—make the moment last.

So here's to the hands that build and mend,
To the early risers, the shift's end.
This place is for you—come as you are,
You're the heartbeat, the fire, the North Star.

Coffee for the calloused, served hot with respect,
No need for a suit, no need to impress.
You built the world—now let me brew
A quiet corner made just for you.

Farm Workers

It's backbreaking work
picking our local bounty
with no help from ICE

Workers of the Fields

In the strawberry fields of Central California
hooded workers bend over rows upon rows
of ripening berries. Raised altars covered in white,
punctuated by broad, brown backs bent to their work.

From the highway, the berries look like little sacred hearts
set on green offering plates as if nature were giving
communion to save our souls.

The pickers look like monks bent in reverence
as they bow and pluck and place
red fruit gently in their boxes for pilgrimage to market.
Sweat christening both ground and berry.

I see only their brown hands rhythmically picking
and packing as if counting beads on a rosary.
Their hoods hide their faces as they work.
Perhaps this priestly order prefers to remain anonymous.

Bow, pluck, place.
Did I hear an "Amen?"
Bow, pluck, place.
Yes. It sounds like, "Amen."

I imagine the pickers chanting to keep time as I roll past:
"La sangre de Cristo,
La copa de salvación.
El cuerpo de Cristo,
El pan de vida."

"The blood of Christ,
The cup of salvation.
The body of Christ.
The bread of Heaven."

World Peas at the Isla Vista Community Garden

—Journal entry, Spring 2004

Longtime Hmong gardeners occupy the east end. They have little to do with the District, but pass their rich soil to family members who keep to the old plantings: Asian pumpkin, coriander, mustard. The Korean gardener built a trellis for his wrinkled chayote. He shared a recipe at last fall's potluck. All the rage, new trellises sprang up. Mexican gardeners plant in rows and ditches: corn, frijoles, chilis, zukes, tomatillos, tidy little farms tended by parents and young children. Students rotate compost, import worm castings, grow vetch to replenish soil. Rich dirt is priceless. The poet sits in a grove of tall mugwort, makes notes and sips comfrey-spearmint tea from a Mason jar. Her sunflowers grow inches per day in a race with nearby asparagus shoots. The French gardener passes cooking herbs over the fence, she trades for aloe. He shows his little daughter how to tell a weed from a crop plant. Now, at the sunset hour, we are ten gardeners (of 28) working happily. Some prune to the sound of weary bees. Others throw water and chat with neighbors. Tomato vines wither in sea air. Who has a remedy? Tabitha's fire-red passionfruit is about to bloom—she tends her paradise of exotics. We sharpen our hoes to battle kikuyu in the sandy back plots. Fauna: Honeybees in comfrey, cat in catmint, scrub jay in sunflowers, topo in carrots and glads, earwig in asparagus, cabbage white in wild ginger, hummingbird in sage, snail in chard, golden carpenter bee in lavender. Red-shouldered hawk, quiet for now, waits on a low post for the gopher to show. Tomorrow we hold a class on complementary plantings. New gate signs are on order. Blue borage stars + multi sweet peas are faves—plant more of these next year!

The Best in Santa Barbara

For an A, I'd write about the pomegranates on my neighbor's vine.
Purple leather outside
Slimy, sweet within.

But, I won't write for grades.
Instead, I'll praise,
the simple meals
on east Ortega.

Spaghetti bolognese, cheese quesadilla, French bread
A vine of grapes, a watermelon, berries
Green cartons of whole milk, and
a bowl of 2% thick grated cheddar.

Food made with love, with hope, with understanding.
Blossomed from the pocket,
the hand,
the heart
of a volunteer.
Swallowed by the stomach,
the hand,
the heart,
of the unhoused.

A warm meal—
the best in Santa Barbara.

My Little Town

My little town is surrounded
By an abounding growth of things
Encapsulated in the greenery
The rivers and the streams

I live among the flowers
I live among the crops
The plants that fill my body
The growing never stops

The tractors till the dirt
So the seeds and plugs
Will be welcome in the soil
Where Gaia gives her love

Yes, the dust lands on my table
Earth lives in my home
As the ground is turned
Making way for things to come

I wipe it away with regard
To its origin and its source
Where the wind blows
To keep pollen on its course

Months of planting and growing
The tender minding of crops
Credit goes to those who toil
The work that never stops

Every day they labor
Bent with arms stretched out
Harvesting what I eat
Even in times of drought

They deserve respect and honor
Doing jobs that most ignore
Just to feed their families
For just a little more

These people are my neighbors
Friends generous and true
We share what we can
What favors we can do

Without each other we'd not survive
We need the give and take
The circle of death and growth
The abundance that we make

Ode to Minha Avó

—For my grandmother

I only remember you standing
in the little kitchen galley,
more like a hallway
where everything happened.
The space was a mere afterthought
to the dance-floor-sized dining room
in the old house where grandfather
lorded over the massive table.

Easter, each year, Mom and I
would come to help you,
hauling in the four-foot-wide
galvanized water tub from the barn.
Clearing it of stray oats and dust,
we mixed the dough and watched in awe
as it rose, making a huge white dome
growing as if by some sacred force.

You made your special *Folar da Pascoa*,
Easter bread for everyone. Everyone.
The basin was big enough to bathe in,
but what covered us was bits of flour
and the commonality of birth.
We pulled and pushed the raw components,
rolling the loopy cords to weave the baskets
tucking a secret celebration of eggs
inside each rising beauty,
thinking our separate thoughts.

I doubled Mom's recipe today
and felt my tired arms while
wondering how you managed
to knock down all those loaves
meant for others.

How did you live your life in that little space,
carrying the burden of all your stillborn babies,
and all the others that survived?
You baked! You gave it all away.

I watched you there, heavy with no adornment,
I saw your strength then, as I see it now,
and I am grateful for the lesson.
You were always in that doorway in the kitchen
quietly giving sustenance to everyone,
out of the way, Avó,
but I saw you.

For Here Please

The models are in good synoptic agreement

The wet morning coffee shop lights flick

There are a dozen crows and two hawks conversating

It is over cast

I have too many thoughts to manage

The incoming front

A weak upper low is spinning along the coast

I still feel like that mother herding her young

Fortitude!

If you can say it you can bear it

Words make it both more real and less alone

I feel a lightning streak of empathy

When the barista clocks out

Air kisses to her coworkers

Now the day is hers.

Harvesting History

The News-Press reported in September, 1950
that because walnut-picking season
in Carpinteria and Goleta Valley was at its peak,
kindergarten enrollment dropped.

Imagine! Five-year-olds fidgeting with burlap
beside orderly rows of trees, while parents'
poles prod tangled branches to make
husk-cushioned walnuts thunk to the ground.

Did the children rush in, like they would for piñata candy?
Were there competitions; did they make it a game?
Or was it tedious, hot, sweaty in Santa Barbara September,
and did they think of missing school with relief, or dismay?

By the time those children graduated high school,
walnuts would give way to lemons and avocados
on the ranches of Hollister, Stow, Ellwood Cooper, and others;
on Chumash land, where oak-forest acorns fell before.

Did those ranching families imagine we'd invoke
their names today, daily in streets, parks, a neighborhood, a school?
Most of us not knowing why, nor giving it much thought
as we take our kindergartners on a field trip to a farm.

Rotten

The tear gas
has dissipated.
A Black Hawk circles
above the fields
where plum trees droop
with fruit that drops
to the ground,
bruised and oozing,
with no one to pick,
or package, or bring it
to the tables
where we shake
our heads
over broken,
empty bowls.

Strawberry Pickers on the Plain

Brushstrokes   color splashed
                    onto a field of dusted green
dabs of purple   orange   yellow—
a pastoral canvas
            from the cool comfort of my car
sweet berries on my tongue
                    bought a mile back

berries picked   out there
with jack-knifed backs   in hours of glare
hoods pulled deep over their eyes
                    hands as rough as bark
Out there—
carmine fruit stains their fingertips like blood.

The Strawberry Guy

A sandwich board with a dancing strawberry
Placed at the corner near the Mobil gas station
Let us know the Strawberry Guy was open for business.
His white truck parked on the street by Trader Joe's
Down the block from the high school.
A facet of local life late April through October most days of the week
He waited in the shade of an oak tree.
Green square plastic baskets of luscious red ripe
Strawberries, now three for eleven
Abundant and sweet flavors of Southern California farm fields.

We used to brag how lucky we were
Our Strawberry Guy a neighborhood fixture.
Once we brought a flat of strawberries on a road trip to Las Cruces.
Another time we served them to our visiting family from Hawaii
An ephemeral gift from our home to your mouth
To nibble and gobble, gossip and quip
Good naturedly in good times.

He's been absent since early June when ICE raided L.A.
Followed by cities and towns all over California.
I never knew his name
And I'm sorry I never asked.
But he was a feature, a highlight, from my corner of the world
Six months out of each year, for many years
Offering a refuge to strangers in sweet delights.

In Lompoc We Do Not Grow the Big Tomatoes

We know better by now.
No Mortgage Lifters, Mr. Stripeys,
or Cherokee Purples.
No beefsteaks or big heirlooms
the size and weight of a heart.

That first year
we had so much hope: we planted them all
in carefully prepared raised beds,
with basil and marigold companions.
Composted, then watered the evenly spaced craters
in the dirt one, two, three times. Wiggled
tiny plant infants from starter pots to tip them gently
into new homes.

Oh, how we cared for them. Pulled off laterals
so the vines would grow like teenagers,
slightly spindly but always upward.
We untangled the tomato cages
when it was time, pushing the wire legs
down. More laterals—we were ruthless.
Even when the suckers grew flowers,
we tore them off with impunity,
never mind the irritation of the green leaves
and stems, itchy fingers for the day.
We watched for aphids and attacked
with soapy water. Swatted the moths with
old tennis rackets, picked the green hornworms off
and put them in the neighbor's yard.

When the wire frames threatened to collapse
we propped them up with stakes. More cages.
Twine and clips. Anything, everything,
like our lives depended on it.

Sometimes the work is not rewarded.
Sometimes the love just isn't enough.
Some places are too cold and windy to grow big fruit.

Oh, the plants would try—fruit would set, and then wither.
Or worse, they would grow, turn color—and then—
a black spot would appear. And grow. We searched the *Sunset* books:
Was it blossom-end rot? Just a squirrel or a jay having fun?

Sometimes, it doesn't matter what the problem was.
Just that it didn't work. Not here.

In the end, only the cherry tomatoes really made it.
Small things, not to be shared, but single-sized bits of joy
to pop in one mouth and one mouth only.

Sometimes life is like that.
Sometimes, the joy is not meant to be shared.
Some people may know why, but that won't be us.
We are resigned, and turn
to Brad's Atomics, the Sweet 100s,
Yellow Pears.
We leave the shared plates of big juicy slices
to other farmers, for other tables.
Sometimes, a single Sungold is enough.

From the Land to Your Table

Take one *pizca* from each *rincón* of the county,
a pinch of Santa Maria strawberries,
another from the fog-kissed Pinot in the Sta. Rita Hills.
Stir gently—nothing of this would be possible
without the families and field workers
whose hands rise before the sun,
whose backs bend so ours don't have to.

Fold in a handful of broccoli crowns
from Guadalupe's endless green rows,
a splash of Viognier from the Santa Ynez Valley,
and just enough humor to keep the pot from boiling over—
because every good recipe needs a laugh,
even if it's only the quiet kind shared
between rows of vines at 6 a.m.

Add birria, tacos, mariscos
from the food trucks on Broadway
and Milpas Street,
drift in their music as an added seasoning.

Let diversity simmer —
California has always been a stew,
and Santa Barbara County knows the recipe by heart.

Now grate in a little Syrah smoke from Ballard Canyon,
a ribbon of Grenache heat from Los Olivos,
and a bright squeeze of Chardonnay sunlight
from the Santa Maria benchlands.

Taste for gratitude.
If it's missing, add more.
There is no such thing as too much.

And just before you're done,
brighten everything with Albariño —
that clear, citrus note
to remind you
light always finds its way.

IV.

Market

Earth Farmer Blossom Market

The mounds of purple eggplants, some
bulbous, others long and narrow,
the rich red San Marzanos, yellow
brandywines, orange carrots
with their bursting ponytails of green,
the staid zucchinis, wrinkled cucumbers,
layered wisdom of paper-skinned
onions, the cheerful mandarins, stolid
apples, leafy moodiness of deep,
dark spinach, the slender loneliness
of green onions—all these vegetables
and fruits bow to us with their bounty.
And so we praise the hands that pressed
their seeds into earth or winter-pruned
their branches, that offered water
to their thirsty roots, protected them
from enterprising green thieves, nurtured
and encouraged them, picked and collected
them, packed them into crates,
and drove them in a coughing van, leaving
before dawn after kissing the sleeping
toddler, the restless husband, peering
through darkness on country roads with only
the radio for company and thoughts of a sickly
mother far away, arriving in the heart
of the city where you and I pause
our busyness to be enriched, nourished
by their very presence, hues of health,
well-wishes of the tended earth,
ambassadors of the rain, carriers of the moisture
that rises from the sea and blesses us all.

Farmers' Market Surrender

Life does go on
for you, for me
and we slog through
on the way towards Saturday.

Like dutiful soldiers
we wipe away sleep
before sun, rise one

by one, and from
all corners, point
our chariots—
charge mercifully

assembling in corner
lots, grabbing
cloth bags like swords
and march

through the gates of heaven.
How easily we fall
out of formation—
with farmers and friends—

as though purple eggplant,
wrinkly brown dates,
crisp green everything,
plump peaches, sweet Valencias
could defeat the week's angst,
bring us to our knees, our stoves
our cutting boards, as we yield
to this otherworldly abundance.

Market

She walks through rows
of green and floral hues,
ticking clocks all around her,
and he does the same, exchanges
one thing for another, currency
for blood oranges and abundant honey.

They move through canopies
of light, the color of sage today,
remembering the need for thyme,
and the taste of summer's apricots,
collecting ways to move beyond
the unsaid, the bounty of worry.

For a short time, distraction is alive,
is allowed to breathe in the concrete
scent of earth, the stock of abundance,
the sweetness of choice at every turn,
exchanging one thing for another, in search
of escape through a bundle of radishes.

Haiku Inspired by Our Beloved Region

Saturday Fisherman's Market

> Morning mist hovers
> Over each catch hauled to shore...
> Our sea's offerings

Hope Ranch Mussels

> Succulent treasures
> Coaxed from protective armor...
> Each to be savored

Downtown Farmer's Market

> The bounty beckons...
> Each purveyor entices...
> A year-round blessing

Jasminum Officinale

> Long awaited blooms
> With intoxicating scent
> Echo summer's lure

Farmers Market Stroll through the June Gloom

I remember to put the raspberries into the glass bowl, to show off the rich color,

As he prefers.

Raw walnuts, chia, and hemp seeds added to steel-cut oats splashed with almond milk. Coffee for me, tea for him. A perfect breakfast.

Wrapped in warm sweaters, we venture out the door into the gray chill over the few blocks to Carrillo and State.

Vendors call out. *Hi, good to see you! A dollar discount for you on the peanuts.*

Jason adds a few extra juicy, ripe apricots.

How much for the cherries? *Today. No charge.* You spoil us! He winks.

As you deserve.

Susan, with the wild dreads, offers a taste of a mixture of spiced nut butter, and a smile. *Thanks!* Smile returned.

Overflowing green baskets of ripe shiny blueberries beckon. Plump ruby red cells of strawberries glisten. Pungent smell of arugula, citrus, and peanut butter surround.

Old and newer friends chanced upon as we stroll between the booths of plenty. Sweet greetings and hugs.

We step lightly into the sunny Santa Barbara afternoon.

Miracle in the Market

It was Saturday, late April air—
Soft sun danced through my flowered hair.
A gentle breeze, light as jasmine's sigh
Whispered sweet nothings as it wound by.

In white dress trimmed with blooming grace,
Heels kissed the pavement, slow in pace.
Crowds turned and smiled while their glances stayed,
Receiving compliments and smiles as I sashayed.

We strolled from upper State, hands tight,
Through Paseo's charm bathed in golden light.
He knew them all, each soul, each name—
And no two greetings felt the same.

We tasted fresh berries, figs, and dates,
Each bite like love that softly waits.
Like my first California sunrise, my spirit was anew—
So ripe, so real, so organically true.

Then I spotted roses blushed in pink and white,
Much like my dress, with the colors just right.
I breathed them in, eyes closed, heart bare,
Love's fragrance swirling in my air.

I turned to see him wink and pay,
"Keep the change," he laughed, and turned my way.
Then, sudden as sound, a kiss became me, bold and pure—
And from that moment, Santa Barbara, I was all yours.

Tuesday Farmer's Market

On a Tuesday evening in late August,
Deidre and I meet to walk the long, sunlit aisle of State Street,
meandering from stand to stand,
where farmers lay out their harvest.

Berries wait, heavy with sugar and fragrant in the heat.
Tomatillos rustle in their papery skins.
Jars of marmalade are stacked,
glowing bright as gemstones in the sun.
We sample slices of apricot smeared with nut butters,
that carry the warmth of the Central Valley.

As we wander, feasting on scent and sight,
we speak of the week just passed—
its knots, its routine joys—
and then, more softly,
we let our dreams spill out too.

Among baskets of figs,
Deidre talks of building a bakery,
selling loaves of brioche as soft and fragile as the fruit.
Rolling a thin-skinned heirloom tomato between my palms,
I admit I'd like to write a book someday,
filled with juicy stories of ocean adventures,
perhaps seeding inspiration for future generations.
Gritty as the dirt clinging to bunches of carrots,
we plan to climb mountains.

It is a communion—
small, ordinary,
yet holy enough to slow us,
to open ourselves to possibility.

What a gift,
to walk beside a friend
through the abundance of the land,
to taste what has been grown with care,
to carry home not only fruit and greens
but also tales of each other's dreams.

The Farmers' Market

Strawberries, juicy, and smelling so sweet,
Shall I buy three baskets, or more, to eat?
Even redder are raspberries, a bit tart for me,
So pretty, I'll concoct a raspberry tea.
Blueberries, plump, with a purple hue,
I'm thinking pancakes, scones…oh, yes … those will do.
Dark shiny red cherries, at last, are in season,
A bag full, please, (I don't need a reason).
These berries are sunshine ready to taste,
Savor each flavor, not one will I waste.

Cherimoyas, (oh boy) … they look so odd,
With a big black seed in a fleshy pod,
And, who can pass up passion fruit, not I,
A delicate taste, a delight to try.
Avocados, red apples, and yellow apricots,
All lovely and healthy, I'm buying lots.
Potatoes, tomatoes, onions … oh, some carrots, too!
Can't wait to get home, for a salad and stew.

Smiles and a nod to each vendor, whose hand,
Shows the stain of the soil from working the land,
Their spirit comes with me, to my home, in my soul,
As I'm nourished with each meal, and bountiful bowl.

V.

RITUAL

And Who Doesn't Love a Good Food Fight?

For 45 years now every August
La Tomatino Festival is held in Spain
Thousands descend on tiny Buñol
    to hurl over-ripe tomatoes at each other

Soft & bursting, red round missiles fly
Some dare to wear white
And some couples even sit on the cobblestones
        and kiss
An irresistible fresh new target

As for me, I'd much rather sauce them than toss them

For my own Festival Tomatino
I cradle tender Heirloom softies
Farmers Market fingerprints still fresh

I chop them with garlic, and more garlic still
  into a pan of sizzling oil
And after 5 hours of simmering to Miles Davis' horn
They reduce to a dense, sweet jam
I ladle onto Farfalle al dente,
  shower with Parmesan Romano
  and reach for Chardonnay sourced from butter & oak

Broad savory flavors perfectly paired with family & friends
Gathered around an endless summer evening al fresco

Fully sated, we roast each other
  and hurl soft tomato insults
  with teasing, loving winks...

Equinox Balm

Tomatoes set
Basil flowers
Night and day are equal hours
Roses bloom in every room
Lettuce bolts
Blossoms are yawning
Grapevine creeps
And covers awning
Birds start singing
Before the dawning
Noontime heats
A sweet siesta
Go to sleep
Until fiesta

Still Wild

each spice
each savory broth

each tender spurting
tomato slippery

silken translucent onion
splattering the front of my shirt

Yes. I embraced deliciousness
and the chatty winemaker next door

who made a generous pour
and read my tongue

like a palm reader
I told him that I preferred Reds—Syrahs and Cabs

and he predicted that I grilled and glazed
my Brussels sprouts sticky with maple syrup

and bacon, please...*remember that?*
How did he know? *Mmm, I'd like another*

somewhere amidst the glinting silverware
and reverent silences I nearly forgot

how I missed rinsing soapy dishes
and waking up alongside you

Oh, to live
among the grape-infused, sun-soaked

unabashedly sensuous
with all their raggedy-torn tendrils
clinging to this still wild earth.

Vices & Spices

Ghostly tendrils of the faintest mist
Rise and twist,
Like serpentine dancers
Or ribbons made of will-o'-the-whisps.

Fine china radiates
Warmth cupped in a supplicant's palms,
The liquid of summer's gold
Aged and cured,
To autumn's honeyed amber.

Breathe deep
The spices of empires,
Earthy, rich, biting, sun-drenched.
With practiced ritual
I lift fall's libation to my lips
And we kiss.

Dinner in the Yard

Driving to your house, worries fly into the rearview on the 101
Ocean is my right hand, mountains are my left
Anxious hum of my inner highway alchemized to presence in the sea salt air
Exiting San Ysidro Road, exiting reality
Or perhaps just entering a better version of it
Jasmine, lemon, eucalyptus
Doors open, arms open, hearts open
Open bottle of bubbles
Mixed with your persimmons, your limes, your scientific brain's
Concoction of dreams
Savored, sandwiched, together on the couch
The yard stretches gracious arms out to the green avocado trees
The golden citrus-soaked mountains coax out life's juiciness
While flames ignite, succulent steak, oversized-just-right burgers,
        tender-as-a-peach halibut
The grill—a turntable spun by a zealous meat-master-maestro
Fresh Oat Bakery bread, a warm familiar friend
You, my warm familiar friends, who need no butter, no salt
For buttery salty generosity, the fat and flavor of life, seeps easily from your hands
From your smiles, as we drink the Los Olivos Cuvee Le Bec you've been saving
But never too long
Dessert? No room, but always room for fresh strawberries
On warm biscuits, pile on the pillowy whipped cream
Tucked in
Under the Santa Barbara stars

The Offering

For Loie and Van

The oak gives itself up slowly,
shedding branches
left like bones on the canyon floor.

I gather them as someone
who knows what the fire demands:
the richness of their bark.

A currency formed from embers,
where smoke curls
on the tri-tips as they sear,
lacing each bite
with a charred sweetness,
born of ash,
and tempered by time.

Taste it,
and you know where you are:
here—Mission Canyon,
these oaks, this fire.

Cooking Tortillas on the Gas Flame

You told me not to flip tortillas with
my fingers. But this was as you were
dropping a tortilla on the gas flame, as
blue-orange tendrils shot to touch the underbelly,
and I crouched to watch it puff: you grabbed the edge
and flipped it quick. "Don't do this with your hands," you said,
and found a pair of tongs for me.
Our prize was speckled black and brown, just burnt enough for taste,
with rivulets of butter and a salty crunch.

Time again your car crawled up the coastline,
loaded down with cakes of spicy chocolate, piloncillo,
and, of course, tortillas. Time again you left.
I missed the massing of the cousins, aunts and uncles
when you left the last: when all the women
took strings of pearls from your treasures,
wore them to the service and talked of you to friends.

But now I stand here at the stovetop, and I
see you standing here, bending down to
watch the browning, bits of black ash
flaking here and there across the freckled yellow surface,
warning me to watch for fire—and I'm twelve again.

I heeded caution then. But I have burnt
my fingers turning corn tortillas with
my hands, like you.

Tortilla Press

At La Super-Rica I stand in line,

watching as the woman plucks from the masa

rough tufts, steaming, fungal, rolled and shaped, then

squashed flat to circular perfection,

slipped from the plastic sheet, and thrown close-packed

on the comal, warm and soft as Play-Doh.

Back home, I buy a press, and find the squeeze

takes years to learn. Rough edges smooth with time.

Today I film myself making tortillas,

and send the clip to the woman I love.

You are making challah for Shabbat.

We are both married, both hungry, both dreaming

of feeding each other.

Tri-Tip Craving

Savory beef tri-tip
brown seared crust with a tender pink center—
Dan's annual summer party featuring his famous tri-tip
with salsa, garlic bread, chili beans—a classic Santa Barbara cookout.
We went year after year.

8 ½ months pregnant with twins,
no pickles and ice cream for me, I needed tri-tip!
We assumed the annual summer party was on, as it was a long tradition.
It was odd that we never got an invitation, but we went anyway.
But when we arrived, there was no BBQ, no picnic, no tri-tip.

We knocked on the door, just to make sure.
Dan's wife said he was away and they were not having the party.
As we must have looked so disappointed, she probably felt so bad.

She must have said to Dan, "Urgent! Pregnant woman's craving!"
Later that day she called, "Dan is back and he is making tri-tip, come over!"
Just for us, they made a late-night dinner.
Well, really just for me.

Sunday Dinners Reconciled

She takes a moment
to remember
the oven door closing,
squeak then soft thud,
a roast sizzling inside.
Her father always did the Sunday cooking.
He pampered the gravy,
dark brown drippings
turning tan when he stirred in the milk.
Peas from a can,
potatoes mashed, baked,
sometimes from flakes.
The table set with flowery Melmac
like wheels on a festive cart.

For a man who as a boy was half-starved
the meal was an achievement:
"My children will not go hungry."
For a child who was sensitive to textures
the meal was a gauntlet
of grizzle and mush.

As she remembers
the kitchen,
the spoon stirring circles,
the knife cutting through,
she wishes she could say
the thank you
that got stuck
behind the meat she couldn't swallow.
She wants to say,
I understand.
And
the gravy—

that gravy
spread thick on a slice of bread,
cut into nine equal squares,
salty, peppery, smooth.
She wants to say,
I'm sorry
that was all I wanted.

Oyster Feast

Our grown sons are home for an oyster feast.
Where once they needed stools to reach the counter,
they now tower over the kitchen island.

Their father teaches them how to use an oyster knife
pushing it into the hinge between the shells
finessing it open with a twist
then running the knife under the oyster
to release it from its home.

They hold the mollusks in towels
protecting their hands from sharp edges and dull knives.
But food this good demands a sacrifice.
Salt water and oyster liquor sting the cuts on their hands.

One son makes a mignonette for the small oysters
dicing shallots, pouring champagne vinegar
while the other chops garlic, melts butter
for basting the large ones on the grill.

When the time comes
we wash up and gather around the table.
Gently lift shells to our mouths
tilt until the delicate meat
sweet and briny
slips onto our tongues.

Going Out After the Writing Workshop

I'm rich and you're poor.
—a fellow writer

I mean, I'm delicate and flaky myself but this guy wants to pan-fry me, he wants to dredge me in the crumbling flour of his skin and cook me in his butter, he wants to traduce my other main hunger, the hunger for my own desire, the hunger for touch. The touch I want. I mean I'm not a starving waif. I've been hungry some years but not like my brother, he was hungry all his life and nothing could fill him. Yes, I've purchased a bag of sweet potatoes with the intention of making it last a week, practiced the art of imaginary food, making it up in gorgeous detail when little existed but I've warned myself standing in front of the warmth of the oven, stroking my breastbone and imagining the red silk and sugar of its flesh, don't do this too much, I said, or anyone who sets out food will be able to tame you. And now here was a trap set for me in an expensive restaurant in west LA by a man older than my father. And I had appreciated his syntax.

I couldn't taste anything in my mouth. My tongue deserted me. No taste. Not one bite more. I blurted out, you can't buy me, which insulted him and he said no, no, no, you got me all wrong, darlin'. And I hate when a man threatens or demeans me with an endearment, a diminutive, with darlin' or honey, so I had to walk. And I've never had trout almondine again. I'm not a total waif either.

Rabbit Stew and Moonlight Too

She was raised on Beatles, Stones, and dreams,
A high school belle in faded jeans.
A cheerleader once, with style and grace,
Now with ranch dirt on her face.

She skinned a rabbit, soft and sweet,
She'd raised it fair for us to eat.
No shame, just pride in what she grew—
Tonight it'd be in rabbit stew.

She fired the Toro, mulch would fly,
Corn and squash beneath the sky.
The garden rows she tilled with care,
With strong tan arms and wind-blown hair.

Her folks had worried she'd be roughin' it
With no real electric lights to read by it.
But sometimes the generator hummed at night,
Or just our hand-rolled candles burning bright.

She chopped up oak to heat the room,
Her Viking cook stove started to bloom.
She stirred the big pot, a smoky bliss—
With beans and corn and her rabbit dish.

Then two neighbors arrived from miles away,
On horses through the chaparral gray.
With their plums and greens and tales to trade,
Under the oaks and stars we laid.

We popped the cork on aged red wine—
From near the hills where cattle love to dine.
The Sanford vintage, full and bold,
With stories from the ranch we told.

Bob read poems with his drawl and tone,
Sally's jam was the keen flavor grown—
We laughed and bragged of our honeybees,
While ranch dogs begged low around our knees.

The candles cast their golden gleam,
We scooped ice cream from the hand-crank machine.
With sweet plum preserves and sage honey gold,
The dogs stood guard—calm and bold.

Then moonlight danced on orchard rows,
We checked the fruit trees in nighttime clothes.
The apples still firm, the apricots soft and sweet,
With hooting owls we'd often re-greet.

We hooted back to them beneath the skies,
With land-grant hearts and star-struck eyes.
On sacred land where good things grow,
We lived this life most never know.

Apologia...in defense of love

for Daniel
Your time 1943-2025, our time 1997-2025

you nourished me with coq au vin
or was it cassoulet?
potatoes au gratin
endive salad
wine
the color of rubies

we met at a dinner party
on Anacapa
close enough
to hear mission bells toll
you cooked
three-courses
under a piano
I fell in love with you
your musical notes
apologetica
dazzled

we made love in your spaceship house
flying under the radar
beneath an Arizona sky
stars exploding
you tied me in knots
cigar smoke lingering
in the desert air

decades later, I fed you like a wee bird
one bite of hospital dry chicken enchilada
all you could muster

you asked for a '53 Bordeaux
we laughed
the stranger who took your order
with us now
there
in that hospital room
our last intimate moments
a butterfly on the door signifying
your transition

Your body shivered like an earthquake
too soon, your mouth agape, limp
eyes closed
breathing...
listening...(they say hearing is the last to go)
to the grinding beat of the oxygen machine
a loud rhythm
drowning out your compositions

no words
coq au vin or cassoulet
just you
just me
the cricket cried softly

Midsummer

It is midsummer, afternoon
The air lies heavy
under a mantle of sun
The breeze soughs
the poplar and the plum
The bees hum
quiet in the softly
fading petals
The poppies hold their secrets in
tight little fists
You can almost hear the
apples ripening
everything suspended
in this sacred moment

Barefruit Doctor

I administered strawberries,
For an attack of reasonable rage against
A God who made genocide and my own crooked heart.
Their rubysweet, spongetart blood, a perfect match.

I used blueberries like pebble markers
To lure myself northward,
From quagmire showing on every screen—into the woods to wander:
Firmly yielding, glazy curl on the tongue.

After the theme park pumped light back through her eyes,
I stopped for roadside peaches—downy like her
Backlit child's forearms cradling surly brow;
Stickytang sugarsun.

Today, I needed cherries, just to make it through
My dry twelve-step to mercy. Bountiful
Sweet beyond reason, purpling like a lover's lips;
Fruit-flesh repair.

Strawberries in Crunchy Cream

Assemble your bowls
blue, green or black
one bigger, two smaller.

Grow some strawberries.
If you spread straw
under the mounds of toothy green leaves
your berries will stay clean
and not be so shy.

Or buy some.

Either way
they are like heart beats
rinse them gently in cool water
pat them
and put them in your bigger bowl.

Stir sour cream
in one of the small bowls.
Spoon brown sugar
regular or raw
in the other.

Grab a strawberry
by its silly green wig
dip it in cream
then dip it in sugar
bite into sugarcrunch
through richness
right into summer.

Eat the whole bowlful.

Lesson from Nature of Santa Barbara

A fable of two trees, apple and orange,
Gracefully standing,

Mosaicing the heavens with branching,
Humbly rooting the earth,

Delightfully getting their water from the nearby spring
With no confrontation or greed,

Drawing their nutrients from the soil beneath,
Sharing the resources for a thousand years,

Different as they both may seem,
No compulsion on each other is ever seen,

Neither demand from one another
To produce the other's fruit or vanish.

The two trees joyfully accept
Each other's uniqueness with no fear,

Humans have failed to do the same,
A lesson to consider from
The apple and orange trees.

Portrait of the Artist as Citrus Grove

Some days, she is an orange blossom
shrill with the aroma of neroli oil,
oversensitive petals
cascading at the slightest tap.

Some days, she is navel oranges
toddler-proud of their outie belly buttons,
flashing them to any and all.

Other days: someone's *media-naranja*,
half of one sundered fruit,
segments spreadeagle,
dewily riven down to the seeds.

After the grafting of the lemon scion
onto the mandarin cutting—
of the Eureka onto the Cleopatra,
of the beauty onto the grief—
she sprouts into a *limón* leaf,
a staple of her grandmother's tisanes
now neglected for its medicine.

One day a year: a batch
of marmalade divvied up between neighbors.

Monthly she sops herself up
into the throbbing hangnail
of a farm laborer
with the fruit-leather face of her uncle Manolo
who died of tomato-pesticide cancers
after harvesting nightshades
in central Florida for a decade, in the 1990s.

She often becomes the withered shoot,
in denial about its death.

Only once: the word
that will emerge
someday
to rhyme perfectly with orange.

Guest of the Land

We've lost patience
/time
to make it from scratch—
not our appetite for the food.

Hunger for the familiar
burrows its soft
head into our shoulders, ridges
undersides with its unfussy beak.

It is old like the song
of paddy fields,
old like missives
of the cloud.

It is keen
for reverence, not
just epicurean taste.

These secrets travel
with bodies.

We are seeking the flavor
of intimacy
that anchors
us into a continuing story.

There is nothing sentimental
about this eating.

It is a matter of survival.

Food exchanges hands
in Santa Barbara parking lots.

Food is comfort and mettle,
measure of
heritage that does not encumber.

This common language
passes between us,
almost absent-minded.

Nothing else need be said.

Once home, we scoop
out the alu gobi and chole
from plastic containers
and heat them up.

Aroma,
home,
wafts among us.

Gujarat is sometimes here,
or Maharashtra, Bengal, Punjab, Bihar.

Specifics of cuisine
consecrate us
back into woven
collective memory.

With care, each meal
sates, a guest
of the land, like us.

Harvesting the Orb

I exit west off the 101,
   on to the two lane shale road
rolling and undulating. I pass
   the windblown, rusted sign:
"Fruits and Nuts,"
   and then the acres
of pastel lichened fronds and orbs,
   their arms reaching up,
dancing into the gun metal Salinas sky.

The roadside riddled shack
   leans into the onshore Monterey winds,
like a last ditch effort to shelter
   Castroville's claim to culinary fame,
crates of thistles with tiny talons
   on the tips of their spoon-like leaf,
the spiny globe that when grilled or steamed
   yields teasing bracts of meat,
just enough to draw you in
   again and again...
and finally the moonscape heart,
   A tiny, buried clay colored bowl,
the motherlode of richness and taste!

History, and evolution,
   taught us this orb is tenacious,
Homer, the Romans, the French,
   seduced by the artichoke,
record how its threatening talon leaf
   and leathery skin eventually soften
in vinegar, sherry, salt and pepper...
   and how its heart,
after the surgery, the weeding,
   the peeling and plucking

the dividing into quadrants…
        can, and should be, savored
with garlic, butter, and mayonnaise,
        (particularly when grilled by
a man in a pith helmet at the Hitching Post)
        lest the delicious trials and tribulations
of its 100 thousand year journey
        be overlooked.

Late for the Feast

Through the gnarled olive trees
Late afternoon sun casts dappled shadows
on a snow-white cloth.
A low bowl of deep-pink peonies
grace the center of a long table
in a garden of late August blossoms.
Artfully sprinkled pomegranate seeds
complement a spread of culinary marvels.
Fresh peaches, thinly sliced melon,
blackberries bursting with juice
are arranged with care
upon a Delft-blue platter.
Plump oysters nest in their shells,
along with cracked crab from the nearby sea,
and small bowls of shiny black olives
march down the center.
At each end sit silver buckets of champagne,
waiting for a quick twist of the wrist,
and a strong arm to dislodge the reluctant cork.
Each cushioned chair is perfectly placed.
Each chair is empty.

Look more closely...
A small red ant wends his way
with care through melon slices.
Oysters have begun to curl at the edges,
while the crab carries a strong scent of yesterday.
Oozing pastries huddle together
In a soft, sticky mass.
Wine sits in pools of warm water,
warm as the afternoon itself.
The guests have begun to arrive,
buzzing with excitement.
A rapidly growing swarm

hovers eagerly in the air,
and descending quickly,
without discrimination,
proceed to enjoy the feast
as it slips sideways
into its slow and infinite cycle of decay.

Gleaning

I take the quiz, read the word, speak the word,
and it rolls off of my tongue as
ah-mond,
like I'm sighing with pleasure
at the remembrance of its crunch.
This is how we say it here, in my part of California.
I can't say it the other way because my face contorts
as if I'm choking slightly on something that tastes bitter.

When I was in sixth grade, a classmate in my Girl Scout troop
came from a family of Japanese farmers.
They let us glean walnuts to sell after their fall harvest
as their way of sustaining the community they loved so well.
We went out on overcast November afternoons
stomping our dark blue Vans through rich soil,
kicking at the leaves to uncover our bounty.

Then we heard how their family had been interned during the war.
The community they loved had stopped loving them back.

I don't know if it was Manzanar they were sent to,
on buses without good brakes, but it seems likely.
I don't know if they had to sell their orchard
or if someone cared for their land while they were gone
or if they only bought it after their release.
I don't know what they ate while they were there,
but inmates recount that going through the mess hall line was
endless meals of moldy Vienna sausage bought in bulk,
mutton stew without spices that stank across the camp, and
cold Jell-O plopped on top of hot rice.
They mostly ate the rice.
Carry a plate to a sick mother and
by the time you got there
the rice had turned brown from the endless dust storms.

I do know that this was how I learned about concentration camps
and that my neighbors down the block had been held in one, for years.

Is it structural racism, or casual racism,
to so readily announce an executive order
that detains people indefinitely, just because you can?

Before we moved to Santa Barbara, my family would drive up from LA
to see my grandparents and to eat at the original Sambo's.
I loved the clever Indian boy
smiling from the colorful storyboards on the wall
who outsmarted the tigers so they turned themselves into butter.
But I didn't understand that the Mama Mumbo pancake platter
had a name that was eyebrow raising.

The owners excused themselves from criticism
by pointing out that their restaurant name
was simply a merging of their two names,
an amusement, certainly not a slur.

I sit on the same bright orange banquettes
at what is now called Chad's, and scan the menu
for pancakes with tiger butter, whipped cream and almonds.

Over my life, I have gathered information bit by bit,
gagging on the parts that I couldn't stomach,
searching for what is hidden, to make sense of this world
until enough of those crumbs lead me home to the truth.

Cabbage Salad

After Stern

On my mother-in-law's last night alive,
200 minutes before she'd drink
a cocktail of narcotics to ease her
into death, I rushed and juggled
and arrived to her goodbye dinner
with the wrong side dish, and
in a surge of inspiration and resolve,
returned home to make a salad—
and I don't know why I took the time
to walk two blocks back and scan
the contents of my fridge, it wasn't
necessary, I'd just dropped off a tray
of grilled mushrooms and peppers,
and marinated chicken was coming
off the grill, I didn't think I'd make
her life more precious, she'd already
said she'd miss the get-togethers
but   somehow   there was
    wonder   thin-slicing
 the cabbage   time became
    finite   each sliver   fell
with purpose   and out the window
appeared   a great   horned owl
that I could hear   but not see.

Restaurant Ritual

—In remembrance of Carol Decanio Abeles

Trust me, I've tried
but have yet to move beyond
fish tacos
So delicious!
Name a restaurant—it's what I'll order
while my friend Carol was determined
to taste-test everything, regardless

We'd meet at least one a month
at Mesa Cafe
always seated in a small booth
in the back, against the wall
near the end of the bar
where raucous drunks
roared and hollered
We never understood their jokes

Our conversations as rich
and deeply satisfying
as crème brùlée—
problems, politics, poetry—any topic
was on our menu, resulting in
uncontrollable laughter

Our friendship lives forever

Now when nourished in this sacred space
I raise a glass
though sometimes only warm decaf—
Even this would make her laugh!

The Bakery by the Shore

People receive communion
The bishop offers the body and blood of Christ
I forget to put my hands out
The wafer gets raised to my face and I stick out my tongue

My pretty auntie and I chuckle
The choir gets louder and so does my laughter
Swaying side to side I think of the last times
I received *la ostia con mi madre*
Limpio las lagrimas de mis cachetes mientras que mastico
The women in white robes offer me wine
I dip His body in the goblet and cocoon it in my mouth

After mass we go to the bakery by the shore
We both order the American Breakfast:
Two scrambled eggs, bacon, hashbrowns, and a buttermilk biscuit, please

As we eat a man enters through the back holding bouquets trying to sell them
My aunt buys a bouquet saying she's going to offer it to my grandmother,
Her mother, on the ofrenda she has in her kitchen

I cut my buttermilk biscuit in half and butter it
Smothering it in jam and I say to her without thinking
Do you feel that the love you have for my nana has changed?
Is the soul connection still there? My mother told me that
El cordón espiritual está ahí, pero el cordón carnal se ha cortado
I sink my teeth into the bacon thinking, translating in my head
The soul cord is there, but the meaty cord has been cut
I laugh at my mother's words, she's the real poet

She's been gone over ten years and a tear falls but no one notices
over the sounds of staff and diners
Auntie forks her eggs as I bite my biscuit, wondering if I had made a mistake
But sometimes we want to talk about the things that we can't
She says, *I love her, but it's different now because I want to talk to her, but can't*

I finish my meal remembering the times I've broken bread with loved ones
And how the last time my mom broke bread with her mama, she didn't know
it would be their last meal together
before nana would return to where she came from.
116

A Life in Strawberries

When berries were in season, my mother
let us dip them into sugar, making what was sweet
even sweeter. Her mother simmered berries
into wine red preserves, juice translucent
as stained glass. It showed up at breakfast
in a shallow cut glass dish. Once when I asked
someone to pass the jam, my grandmother
explained those pillows of fruit deserved
their own name. After all, a mere taste is all
it takes to recall a child's sticky contentment.

Years later, needing cash for college,
I answered an ad for pickers. An old bus
collected us at first light, took us to the fields
where we bent over rows of tangled vines
studded with rubies. We were paid a pittance
per box. I wasn't fast enough to make
much money, but I never ate another strawberry
without wondering who had done the picking.

We raised our children in a flat, midwestern town
where a dilapidated farmstand claimed to sell
The World's Best Strawberries. The town even had
a Strawberry Festival with carnival rides
and paper plates mounded with crushed fruit nestled
between shortcake slabs and whipped cream clouds.
The year I volunteered, they had me up to my elbows
in cold water rinsing scarlet berries that bobbed
as happily as the berry-stained children running free
with their friends in the endless summer twilight.

Now I find myself on a coast, where even the names
of the berries are delicious—Gaviota, Seascape,
Diamante, Monterey. Like me, these berries thrive
where it is warm but rarely hot. We draw in
morning mist and wait serenely for the sun
to melt it away. Together the berries and I ripen
at our own pace, memories swelling juicy and sweet.

Where Are My Arepas?

Oh, Santa Barbara…fraught with expensive food.
We pay for the weather and idyllic beach views.
Blessed with great agriculture,
but SB! You're missing the foods from my culture!

A Venezuelan, raised in South Florida.
Wondering where's the food from my origin?
Ordered a Cuban Sandwich once, it was missing *jamón,*
y se me partió el corazón.

And SB! Where are my Arepas?
A versatile corn-based flatbread.
You can eat it in the morning with a side of eggs and butter spread.
Or have it for dinner stuffed with a creamy avo guac and shredded chicken.
We call that *una Arepa de Reina Pepiada.*
Imagine a late night Arepa place a few blocks from Granada?

But the lack of my food has its perks.
'Cause look at me, now I am the cook.
I'll make some *caraotas donde tus taste buds explotan*
I'll make a white rice *con sofrito* so fragrant, you'll want to bask in its steam
I'll make *plátanos maduros tan dulces y caramelizados,* you think you're eating candy
I'll make *carne mechada* so tender, chewing is not mandatory
If you put those all on a dish, you'll have Venezuela's national dish,
Pabellón Criollo.
I will enjoy that dish *con Venezuelan orgullo*

So thanks SB for not letting me,
forget me.

Poetry on Platters: A Four-Course Meal of Meaning

Appetizer
Deep-fried, bite-sized sounds,
crisp words,
crack, crunch, and tap
at the skull
as we gnaw, nibble, mull
on thoughts quick and small.
We dip bits in sauce,
slipping sententious new flavor
into the mix.

Soup
Round sounds abound in the bowls brought forth:
Slick streams of sounds, seep warmth into pores
as they're poured, steaming, from silver ladles into ceramic.
Scooping soup onto spoons, we smell the subtle sentiments of the chef.
She has spiced it with sprigs of parsley, covered it in cream—
all to ease our swallowing of bitter criticisms with our thin saltines.
It slides smoothly down our throats, settles into our stomachs.

Main Course
Plunked with hefty thunk onto mahogany is the cast-iron pot—Le Creuset
        —of broiled outcry.
A tangle of scents escape with a smothering cloud of scalding steam, hissing
        as the lid is lifted.
After endless days of roasting, brewing and stewing in a careful concoction
        of concepts—
onions of sharp opinions, many-layered,
meaty portions of ponderings simmering against hot peppers of passion,
salt and garlic-flavored satire sprinkled sparingly 'twixt carrots and potatoes
        of compassion—
the dish, delightfully and dangerously digestible, insists on our consumption.
We stomach all we can, feasting 'til we risk retching, teetering
on the edge
of eating too heavy a spread.

Dessert
Sweet, sprightly relief surges in us as
our plates, still stacked high with savory goods, are whisked away.
Saucy silverware and platters are replaced
with small, clean sets:
Glasses filled with cold, creamy comfort sparkle before us.
Calming cups of tea wait warmly at our fingertips,
and we sip them slowly,
contemplating the content of each course.

VI.

INGREDIENTS

Lemons

Neruda already wrote this poem:
Each tree a dark universe studded
With glowing elliptical planets,
The cut fruit a cathedral, the rind
A goblet of brilliant memory—
I'm paraphrasing translations—
Inhale... Eureka, pink Eureka,
Lisbon and Meyer, Bearss
And Ponderosa—aren't even
The names delicious? Isn't
This tartness refreshing?
Don't we say "Pucker up,"
When we want a kiss? *Gold*
Of the universe, Neruda
Gushed, but it's the gold
Someone believed would
Fall into Spanish hands
We have to thank. Think
Lemon seeds like tiny life
Boats ditched, among other
Goods, so ships could load
Holds with living people—
Kidnapped, shackled, enslaved—
Comercio, trata..."trade":
To the country called, later on,
"America," Columbus brought
This sour fruit. But the varieties
Squeezed above the glittering
Skin of a fish or set like a rose
Window on the edge of your
Icy drink are hybrids, grown
From shoots sent to Sherman
Stow in the 1800s, which his son,
In his "lemon lab," tinkered with:

Varying the rootstalk to generate
Orchard-wide skies of glossy dark
Green leaves gleaming with yellow
Stars. Light we can reach for, hold,
And inhale: bitter light we can
Slice, squeeze, sugar, and gulp...
I could end the poem there, yes?
Spit out history's hard urgent pips
To make it easier to swallow
The present's juicy, acid, pulp?
Delicate Merchandise, as Neruda
Put it: every harvest dependent
On sunlit luck and the life force
That leads these hands deep
Into the grove, and lets the tree
Take for its own the tender graft.

After Lee Young-Li's "Persimmons"

Love rain-scented ghost,
sits in his grave shadow of love,
river of emotions, children,
cardinal songs remembering forgotten
memories, persimmons.

(Jane Gillett)

Golden glowing persimmon,
bright sun. A cardinal by the bedroom window.
Blind sadness, heavy love.
The ghost of the Chinese apple.

(Charlie Schultz)

I didn't eat, but I watched
my mother stay up for days
watching a ghost
a cardinal sat on her windowsill
filled with sadness...I finally understand.

(Quyen Casey)

A Chinese apple locked away
in a stone cold cellar.
But the apple was something golden,
glowing, wanting to be freed,
wanting to spread its joy to all.

(Utah Roth)

In the cellar I found a golden glowing persimmon
on the windowsill. The cardinal was protecting
it with a ghost-like song,
protecting it with its love.

(Nora Frei)

Avocado Days

I would like to put my hand
out to pick you from a tree
and think about those summer days.

Peel back the layers
to a time when skin
felt a little newer to the air.

The rite of passage
mashing guacamole
inviting people over
before the sun
lengthened the shadows.

It was those swimming
spots before your eyes
and the temperature
of just after lunch
that seemed to melt away
one after another.

But today I try to stay green
with a little lime
a dash of heat
the days that have less beginnings
foggy sweater mornings
reaching for muggy afternoons
and ending with the soft
impact of the canyon breeze.

Figs

Fig tree, *santa higuera*,
altar to summer's holy fruit.
Soft, sunburnt tears—
lágrimas para lo que está pasando.
Ancient leather pouches
warm to the touch, time-old
symbol of peace and prosperity.
Higos, your uniqueness inspires,
bundle of hundreds of flowers
turned inside out.
Your taste is divine,
eternally taking me back,
el mar Mediterráneo,
another lifetime.

Tiramisu,

you came from the heart of Italy, you have traveled so far,
through the sunlight and the shining moon.

You are like fall leaves falling,
soft and graceful.

You were born in the kitchen of an Italian chef singing along
to his favorite song, having fun.

Tiramisu, you feel like home.
You remind me of my aunt and uncle.
My Aunt Weiyin brings out the best in you.

You are soft and you can light up any room
with your beauty.
I've always wanted to go to Italy,
you make me feel like I am there.

Your colors are red, white and green,
the colors of your country's flag.

Painted Lady Bean, Improved

Phaseolus coccineus

At the kitchen table,
always solo this early, I sit
to the sunrise, prey
to what could be made
of the day. Shadows
lengthen from the salt
& pepper shakers. I hold
still, wait for desire to move in.

At my elbow a packet
of beans I mean to plant:
Painted Lady, Improved—
and who wouldn't want
that version—early
bloomer, young pods
eaten whole?

Ode to Basil

I worship at your stems!
Your delicate flowers, fragrant
air. You are like money—
green, and one can ever have enough of
you. My grandfather taught me that,
standing in his kitchen, snipping ribbons into
a heap. We were chopping
tomatoes with precision, each a
square and red onion. He sliced the baguette
with the ruler of his eye, surgical
in everything he does, each slice
brushed with olive oil. *La casa nasconda,*
non ruba. His house does not dare
hide anything from him. Only
god can rob my grandfather.
His *moglie.* My Nana. These basil leaves
we would give them all
in exchange for her.
There isn't enough in the world.
I breath in their fragrance each time
I am in the store—I can't seem to keep
them alive at home. Perhaps
I give them too much—too much water
too much sun too much heat too much love—
they will not stay longer.
Linger on my fingertips like garlic,
perfume me with your intoxicating scent
when I go to sleep tonight
I'll dream of you.

Hollister Ranch Honey

—For Kathy & Rick Sawyer

There is nothing quite like it
on a slice of a toast, or stirred
into a cup of hot tea, although

I prefer it straight from the clear
glass jar where its light gold purity
shines like morning sun on the hills

above Little Drake Beach. I dip
a spoon into the alluring stuff,
and the taste travels from my tongue

to my brain, then outward
to my fingertips and toes, the way,
I imagine, opium must singe

every last cell of the body with pleasure.
It is always gone much too soon,
sometimes in a single day.

Because I never know when I will have
more, I ought it savor it, but anything
this good was not meant to last.

Abalone Good Times

At twenty, we didn't know we had questions
but the answer to everything was the beach.

Agitated minds and conflicted hearts were soothed
in the cold Pacific. The sun melted away most grievances.

Beach volleyball and throwing frisbees helped
and the barbecues at day's end resolved the rest.

We'd wait for low tide, search algae-covered boulders for abalone.
No need to dive deep to find them, plentiful back then.

After we gathered enough to feed us all and make a rich broth,
many hands cleaned and pounded the mollusks thin.

Vague memory of what came next—something
to do with seaweed, and lots of butter and garlic.

A beer run was in progress. Pot permeated the air.
Somebody brought lemons and avocados from their yard.

Bread arrived for sopping up everything. Soon everyone's
elbows and fingers were jostling for abalone broth.

Eating, laughing, singing until our bodies, minds
and spirits surrendered to the night.

Lilikoi

People don't know who you truly are.
They overlook you for being gross-looking.
They don't know who you are.
Then when I tell them,
they say, "Passion fruit?"
NO.
Your name is Lilikoi.

People don't see it. They see how you were renamed.
Not the part of you I see.
Purple wrinkles like a grandmother's hand,
and cut open, yellow goo, slime-like, a jellyfish.
Sweet as a honeysuckle.

You remind me of Hawaii.
The warm rain pouring down on my hair.
A soft sweet breeze of ocean water overlapping on my feet.
When I slurp down the sweet goo inside you,
I feel summer.
I jump up and down, when I see you at the market.
I plead and plead until I can feel
the wrinkles of the peel in my hands.

You are my fruit.
I really can't overlook. Never.
I always need you.
I feel happiness
sitting in my mouth.
Like a sweet summer day
I won't ever forget.

Peach

You are a child of summer.
I hear you crying
as if you can
climb back up
to the sky
into God's arms.

Here in the palm
of my hand
you roll as if smiling.
You are getting used
to me.

Soft as my cheek
barely furred
pink and orange
you remember the tree limb
where you started from seed
and grew each day.
As green leaves
fanned you
you became plump
and juicy.

You are falling asleep
in my palm.
I will not take a bite of you.
I will not taste
your sweet flesh.

As I wash your body
you wake.

I towel dry you
and place you in the cool
refrigerator.

I set up a canvas.
Squeeze out paints.
Take you out
and place you on a plate.

As you pose
I lift my brush
and begin your portrait.

After my son eats you
and licks his lips
my painting hanging
on the wall
reminds me
of how plump, colorful
and soft you once were.

Santa Barbara Meyer Lemons

Meyer lemons blush in the California sun, their skins thin and almost translucent, as if holding light captive. They dangle from backyard branches, sprawling groves, where the Pacific breeze meets the scent of citrus. I hold one in my hand and marvel at its softness, how it yields to gentle pressure promising less tart juice than most. Meyer lemonade sold me my last house, served by the homeowner in her backyard orchard. The Meyer lemon continues to be my muse, as in restaurants, the zest perfumes cakes and brightens vinaigrettes while it turns water into sunlight. The taste lingers on, way beyond each sip. You will never forget it.

bursting with lemons
the color of the new sun
early morning detox

Avocado

Hand grenade with its pin already pulled
Once plucked from the grocery store shelf
An audible ticking begins
Tick
Tick
Tick
Tick
Boom

You have been on my kitchen counter for what seems like the blink of an eye
And you are already threatening to rot
To bear witness to the fact that I don't have my act together
That I am hanging on by a thread
That I can't handle responsibility
I can't even manage to eat an avocado

So I don't buy you
I avoid that side of the supermarket
because from it emanates a low hum that sounds like a laugh
Even the granny smith apple
The most stable and forgiving of produce
knows that it will rot in the back of my fridge
Yet continue to stay there
Rotten
For God only knows how long

If only I could sew together the edges of my life that keep me this way
But not today

If Steelhead Is on the Menu

Eyeing you above the crest of a menu
Newly printed today
I am decided

Imagining butterfly cuts
Thanking gods for indignities
The suffering of beasts all in their time

Our liminal wildness

A trout hatched in Arroyo Hondo
Dreaming of movement
It wended its rainbow torso downstream

It kissed a stone
Knew salt for the first time
Remembered it always

Hurling into ocean unafraid
Swallowing whole and new
The trout lost memory of its mother

To become a mother

The taste is evidence
Of crossing
Of exiting and arriving
Of muscle and fat and ligament

From line or net
From icebox or transcontinental hull

To knife
To fire
To dish

Your skin in the moonlight off the sea
The skin of your face in the tealight

Looks flecked and marbled like a trout

You are a prism
More lustrous than your usual luster
Ripe with sheen

Glistening in citrus dew
Earthy sweet like dill and tarragon

Another time it would be my privilege to bone-scale-clean
To pierce-skin-butcher for you

To devour with you
To forget what we have devoured

Oh the embellishments to these lives

Forager Field Guide

The solar system aligns
as king tides bless
December rain
and *Psilocybes* sprout
in the usual places

Candy caps cluster
beneath an elder oak
near a spread of witch's butter
pale deadwood oysters
and black trumpets

My secret stand
of chanterelles—gone
A careless geocache
plain as day, lured throngs
to log *Kilroy was here*

We tramp like boars
by the earth churned trail
at our own risk
Boots slur, paws imprint
the slick sludge

Coming upon a deer spine
set my hairs on end
Lions, tigers and bears
Not to worry
There are no tigers here

Fuchsia-Flowered Gooseberry

(Ribes speciosum)

I don't see any geese around.
So what do they mean, *gooseberry*?
As if my most delicious parts
sprang from the ass of a gander.

And *fuchsia-flowered*? What kind
of a foo-foo farce is that? As if
I were a centerpiece at the annual
luncheon of the Ladies Garden Club.

But my spines and thorns
all along my crooked stems—
these they can't touch.
Hands off! I tell them.

Keep your fancy tongues away!
At least I have something of my own,
something that will make you bleed
all over your white lace tablecloth.

Passion Fruit—The Essence

Passion fruit is the most royal purple.

Its fierce dragon's dark scales,
the seeds are the fire burning
a yellow, orange color.

Passion fruit takes me to France,
to the top of the Eiffel Tower.

Passionfruit skips down the chic streets of Paris,
runs down the normal red carpet
wearing a tipped crown.

A volcano erupting in my mouth
the fragrance of a rose.

Late Summer Fruit

My neighbor brings me fruit
from her garden
figs and passion fruit
I study the beauty
of these delights
the uncountable number
of tiny yellow seeds
embedded in the soft red flesh
of the figs hugged close
by their purple skin.
They crunch like fine grit
against my teeth
but I am not displeased
thanks to the sweet velvet softness
of the bed in which they lie.
I relish the sweet tart juice
inside the purple carapace
of a passion fruit.
The seeds form a perfect triangle
and swim like disembodied fish eyes
in their pool of yellow juice.
All a person needs to do
to enjoy that mouth-puckering liquor
is slurp the whole thing down
like eating an oyster.
It's like returning to the Garden of Eden
but my neighbor's garden is
the true garden of delights.

Ahoy Bok Choy!

Ahoy Bok Choy!
(And you too tomato and avocado and all)
From distant shores you migrated here
Finding space in local farms and gardens
The warm wet winters welcoming
Your growing roots and shoots.
I saw you in markets and wondered
What people you nourish and nurture
What flavors of well-cultured worlds.
When I finally brought you home
I was distraught
Danger coursing through my blood
A time to learn supervenient vitality
To open my soul to newfound sustenance
Embrace a palette of transplanted nutrient wisdom.
So you became my culinary discipline
A cheerful chore of domestic integration
With gratitude for your journey to my big table.

Avocado

Santa Barbara's favorite fruit,
Rich and creamy, it's a beaut.

Mash them up and make them spicy.
If they're grown here, then why so pricey?

In gazpacho or a shake.
Add one to your lunchtime break.

Draped across expensive toast.
So sublime, you'll have to post.

This green orb, I got one gripe.
When the heck is this thing ripe?

On the counter or in a bag.
I've aged a year, it's such a drag

I added an apple to make it faster.
In that time I got my master(s).

Unripe unripe it's still hard.
Should I keep or just discard?

Not ripe not ripe still a rock.
Startin' to think this thing's a crock.

Checked it daily, one day forgotten.
Only to find the darn thing's rotten.

The Orchard

It is grapefruit
she misses, not the apples

despite the years
of picking and pies,

despite the pleasure
of crunching ripe red Envies
warm from California sun.

No, it is the grapefruit

their smooth pink
puckered yellow
skin holding tight

the unexpected
weight of fleshy fruit,

a softened shot put
that fits in her hand,

or a pitcher's perfectly aimed ball
snug in a catcher's mitt

rolling easily, undamaged,
into her wide wicker basket

as she considers
their potential as artillery
against an angry
older brother.

Those reliable yellow globes
that don't lose form,

don't split like peaches
allowing in pesky ants,

don't fail to produce
like the scant avocado

or drop too soon and disappoint
like furry unripe apricots.

The gallant grapefruit tree,
thick with jagged leaves

consistent, prolific,
asking only for occasional

water—its purpose
spilling into her own.

Ramen

You are round like the earth
and have the ocean in your bowl.
You bring a purpose with a smile.
You take me skydiving on fireworks.
You bring a rainbow on a cold foggy day.
You're the feeling when you're on the couch
watching your favorite movie.
You are the feeling of freedom.

Miner's Lettuce

As kids we pulled Miner's lettuce
by the handful, leaves round as toy plates
like edible lily pads
crunch sweeter than iceberg

ramping the banks
along San Antonio Creek
monopolizing oaks' shade
greens tender as bok choy

Miners, hungry-handed invaders
piled their empty pans
like platters
of green gold

gathered leaf
by leaf
earth tinged
exuberant

Toss with red onions
Cucumbers, shaved
carrot, olive oil, lemon juice, a sprinkle
of toasted pine nuts

How can anything so far-flung wild
be so luscious?

Writing Permission as Persimmons

Because seasonal excess becomes an insistence—
Eat Me! Drink Me! demands of our Wonderland—
persimmons clamber from branch to kitchen counter
as if there were a winter here worth hiding from.

Little suns in the months of long nights. Orange not-citrus,
crisp not-apple, radiant in one of Pascale Beale's plated
mandalas. Was Sinatra's "Orange is the happiest color"
an ode to the persimmon?

              As Bouchon's autumnal salad:
crisp fuyus with burrata, bitter endive, and hazelnuts.
In the restaurant's candlelight, crisp slices of fall.
Or is it you and I glowing, despite the burning world?

At home the heart-shaped Hachiyas, too hard and tannic to use,
turn to ripe jelly inside thick skin, then quickly rot. What keeps
trying to teach me patience? The persistent wish for persimmons
when the trees in the neighborhood are naked branches
seasons away from their fruit.

Mangos

The beach ball of sweetness.
The tang zings like lightning, Shiny yellow gold.
A red dragon in the mystical island.
Crisp palm leaves bathed in honey, Eternal and
Everlasting. Morning beach waves in the distance.

In Praise of *Cantharellus californicus*

How I dream to learn some
equivalent, effortless thankfulness,
when I consider California's official state
mushroom, the golden chanterelle.

It and our coastal oaks worked out
a symbiosis—and then after rare rains —
the ridged, whorled trumpet of fungus
brilliantly blooms. You can't count

on them, just hope as you walk the woods
with a wish to forage. Or offer dear cash
at a farmers' market, almost exclaiming
as if seeing a long-missed sorority sister

when spying them piled on tables
the first time each season. Winter has
its delicious privileges. Cooking them is
a lesson in getting out of the way—just

butter, the bite of fresh green garlic,
white pepper to warm as gently
as you can. Splurge with precious truffle
salt, gilding the umami lily. Serve atop

the magic your wife can do with "00" flour,
egg yolks, elbow grease, the genius
of an Atlas pasta machine. Definitely
don't forget fresh tarragon, thyme,

the delight of dusting with Parmesan.
Even the too damn early December
dark can't dim the savoring of simple
warmth and rich and earth and awe.

Ode to Sungolds

In the dormant & dustiest corner
of my yard, amid the slow wilt
of weeds, a new creeper appeared
overnight.

The thing grew & grew, lit the place
a bright new green, until, one noon,
the sun hit a golden glow —
                      a tomato!

A thumb-sized & plump & round
& perfectly ripe little thing. Then ten,
then more. *They're Sungolds*, coughed
my old neighbor, *shat by a bird*.

So, here's to butter & olive oil, garlic,
basil, oregano & amber bursts, all a-
sizzle in my skillet. What blessings —
straight out of bird shit.

Oysters

I must have been seven that day my father pulled off the highway
to the shop in Morro Bay that sold shucked oysters by the quart.
Outside on the street, he tilted back his head gulping them down
like a seal. When he insisted I try one, it came right up. Unable
to recall his exact words, I imagine he was concerned I'd wasted
a perfectly good one. Something like, *Oysters don't grow on trees.*

By the time I was twenty-two I'd grown to love them, their sharp,
gritty shells, the smell of brine and seaweed, the forever elusive
prize of pearl. A lover fed me with a tiny silver fork—they slipped
down my throat in a wash of champagne.

In Paris, with my husband, oysters arrived on a three tiered platter,
glittering cold in their icy bed. The were *Huîtres à Volant*, "flying
oysters" freshly harvested off the Normandy coast.

And, in a harbor restaurant in our town, the bartender jimmies
his blade into a tight-lipped shell, then plops the oyster
in a shot glass filled with vodka and horseradish. You are expected
to swallow the concoction down in one gulp—and I do.

Thank God Alligator Pears Aren't Sold

by weight like gold.
                    Cue ball seeds
                with minds
       of star-fondling height,
       blue shade width,
       & obscure web-depth   ready

to succumb to the rumba
       of charmed bees, the orchestra of fickle rain.
Crayon-green leaves like ellipses inhale us—sighs
      & all.
          How Does It Know
Avocado—the word descends from the Nahuatl —
        ahuacatl.

I'll let you look it up —

Close Encounter with Basil

Walking past my basil plant
my pant leg makes gentle contact
releasing a pungent, enticing fragrance
and suddenly I am in wine country
on a languid afternoon savoring
a baguette with an assortment of cheeses
and pesto so satisfying
lovely tannins in a sensuous red wine
valley oaks on a golden hill

I forget what brought me out to the patio
Perhaps reclining in the nearest chair
will help me sustain this reverie

Randy Arnowitz, or "Mr. Greenjeans," as he has been known in Santa Barbara since 1982, is a professional rosarian, garden writer, horticulturist, and gardener. Most days he can be found with his beloved doodle, Maisie, deadheading, feeding, watering and fawning over the many rose gardens he tends in Santa Barbara. He has written for *Edible Santa Barbara, The Santa Barbara Independent, Montecito Journal, The News-Press* and oh yeah, *Weird New Jersey,* among other publications.

Alison M. Bailey studied poetry with James McMichael at UC Irvine and Suzanne Lummis at UCLA. She won the Glenna Luschei Poetry Contest in 2016. Her poems appear in *Sage Trail, To Give Life a Shape, Rattle, Miramar,* and *Elsewhere, Paradise* (Santa Barbara poets respond to paintings by Patricia Chidlaw) and were featured in "From Verse to Visual." Her novel *XP*, about the Pony Express, was published in 2012. She launched a virtual reality app called "VR Guest" which is an experience of dining with Kleopatra, Mozart, and Einstein. She lives in Carpinteria with her rescue dog and an abundant avocado tree.

Lisa Bass lives in Santa Barbara where she writes poetry and short prose. Her work appears in *Ninth Letter* and *Willow Springs,* among others, and has been selected as a *CRAFT* Literary Editor's Choice and a *Rattle* Poetry Prize finalist. Lisa works as a social impact consultant, facilitator, and leadership coach; and studies and teaches at the Writers Studio.

Emily Bernhardt is retired from numbers and Los Angeles. She lives in Ventura and commutes regularly to Santa Barbara to volunteer at the Botanical Garden and meet her friends for lunch at Jeannine's. She is also happy to share a meal at Maíz Picante Taqueria—name the time!

Kit Bonson is a neuroscientist in the Santa Barbara area with degrees in English and psychology. She has been an activist for peace, justice, and reproductive healthcare rights for 45 years. As a Board member of the social justice poetry organization Split This Rock, she founded their Annual Abortion Rights Poetry Contest. She grew up in Southern California and has been writing poetry since she was a child. Her poem "Periplum" was published in *Beltway Poetry Quarterly.* This year, a quince tree in her backyard gave her amazing and unexpected fruit!

Laure-Anne Bosselaar authored five poetry collections, is the recipient a Pushcart Prize, and the James Dickey Poetry Prize. She edited five anthologies & served as Santa Barbara's Poet Laureate (2019 to 2021). *Lately, New & Selected Poems,* came out from Sungold Editions. She loves Sungolds. And fries with mayo, with a cool glass of Awesome Possum beer.

Gudrun Bortman grew up in Hamburg, Germany. She is an artist and a garden designer. Her poems have been published in various magazines and anthologies. Her chapbook *Fire Weed* was published in 2018.

Alison Brysk is a professor at UCSB and the author of eight books of non-fiction. She is the mother of two young women and has traveled to 55 countries. Brysk has lived in Santa Barbara since 2011, where she worships at the Saturday Santa Barbara Farmer's Market.

M. L. Brown is the author of *Call It Mist*, winner of the Three Mile Harbor Press Book Prize, and *Drought*, winner of the Claudia Emerson Chapbook award. One of her favorite local foods is the sweet fruit from her backyard tangelo tree.

Christopher Buckley's *Sprezzatura* is published by Lynx House Press, 2025. His work was selected for Best American Poetry 2021, and he is the recipient of a Guggenheim Fellowship in Poetry, two NEA grants, a Fulbright Award in Creative Writing, and four Pushcart Prizes. *One Sky to the Next*, was winner of the Longleaf Press book Prize for 2022. He has edited over a dozen critical collections and anthologies, most recently *Naming the Lost: The Fresno Poets—Interviews & Essays*.

Nic Caldwell doesn't eat to live, she lives to eat! Nic holds a MSt from the University of Oxford. Her academic focus was culinary archaeology and the far-reaching repercussions the Indo-Roman trade had on cuisine around the world. Nic has lived in fourteen cities and six countries, but feels she has finally found "home" in Santa Barbara. A master chef's daughter and NorCal native, Nic loves to cook and explore the Central Coast's culinary scene. Her favorite Santa Barbara restaurants include Alessia Patisserie for breakfast, Happy Cat Eats for lunch, Secret Bao for dinner, and Creaminal for dessert.

Jose María Carpizo was born in León, Guanajuato, Mexico, and moved to Santa Barbara in 1985. His love of poetry began with his art appreciation classes in high school by his teacher Christian Jean. One of his great influences was his father reading about poets of the 1952 generation from Spain. He continued his learning with workshops here in Santa Barbara and in Mexico. He is presently in a workshop hosted by Laure-Anne Bosselaar. His favorite dish is mole, favorite condiment is achiote, and favorite wine is Pinot Noir from Santa Rita Hills.

Carolyn Chilton Casas has lived most of her life on the central coast of California. She is a practicing Reiki master who explores ways of healing in the articles she writes for wellness magazines. Her poetry has appeared in *Braided Way*, *Grateful Living*, *ONE ART*, and *One Earth Sangha*, and in anthologies including *The Wonder of Small Things*, *Thin Spaces & Sacred Spaces*, and *Women in a Golden State*. More of Carolyn's work can be found on Facebook or Instagram, on www.carolynchiltoncasas.com, and in her newest collection of poetry, *Under the Same Sky*. She loves to eat sun-ripened fruit.

Quyen Casey is a 6th grade student at Mountain View Elementary. Quyen loves to sketch, listen to K-Pop—particularly Stray Kids—dance and play with her dogs, cat, and goats. Her favorite food to make at home is mac-n-cheese with steak bites. Poetry helps Quyen with sorting out her thoughts.

Susan Chiavelli's chapbook *Alas...* is forthcoming from Finishing Line Press. She is the recipient of the *Chattahoochee Review*'s Lamar York Nonfiction Prize for "Death, Another Country," also named a notable essay by *Best American Essays*. Her award-winning prose and poetry have appeared in *The Los Angeles Review*, *SALT*, several Shoreline Voices anthologies, and elsewhere. Susan's favorite drink is one she invented, A Good Lion made with Gunpowder gin.

Clayton E. Clark is a poet, painter, wife, and mother who studied Art History at UCLA as an undergrad and worked more odd jobs than can be counted. She also worked at the Otis/Parsons College of Art and Design for years before having kids. She loves to hike, swim, explore museums and dabbles in playing guitar. Publications include *SALT*, the anthology *While You Wait*, and *Anacapa Review*. She has been awarded *Rattle*'s Prompt Poem of the Month.

Evelyn Cox is a 6th grade student at Mountain View Elementary. Evelyn loves being in water: surfing, skiing, swimming, tubing. Evelyn loves the comfort of her mom's lasagna. She loves how poetry gives her the freedom to express her feelings.

Sharon Cox is a reader and sometimes writer of poetry. Newish to Santa Barbara, she continues to discover those places that inspire and people who enrich life.

Kimberly Ferris Crocker is a recovering financial expert, diplomat, writer, dancer, foodie, and seeker of truth. She began writing poetry in 2015, after the sudden death of her younger brother. Her work has appeared in *Adelaide Literary Magazine* and in the Adelaide Literary Award Anthologies of 2019 and 2020. Kimberly lives in Santa Barbara with her husband, two children, and a small menagerie of animals collected from around the world. She often frequents the local farmer's markets and has an addiction to California's fresh produce and seafood.

Susan Read Cronin is a broccoli lover and could live forever on bacon fumes. She grew up in an area where feasting on ethnic food meant opening a can of Chung King Chicken Chow Mein. Having eschewed "alligator pears" as a child, she discovered her passion for avocados when she moved to Santa Barbara full-time in 2016. Besides having written three books of poetry, Cronin is known as a bronze casting sculptor of animals, who often turns her hand to vegetables in an attempt to divine emotions from them.

Ruben Lee Dalton was born and raised in Southern California. In 1966, after high school, Ruben enlisted in the Marine Corps and subsequently spent 14 months in Viet Nam. During his tour of duty Ruben started documenting his wartime experience with poetry and letter writing. Following his military experience he attended UC Santa Cruz for his undergrad education, and UC Berkeley for his graduate studies. Over the years he has published poetry and short stories in various journals and anthologies. He currently lives on a ranch in North County Santa Barbara with his wife and many animals.

Fran Davis is the author of the historical fiction novel *Red Summer* (2025). Her poetry, essays and short stories have appeared in *SALT, Calyx, Chattahoochee Review*, the *Hopper, Vincent Brothers Review, Reed Magazine, Passager*, and several Gunpowder Press anthologies.

Pamela Davis is the author of *Lunette*, winner of the ABZ Poetry Award in 2015. Additional recognition includes two Pushcart nominations, finalist for the American Literary Review Poetry Prize, and two-time finalist for the Pablo Neruda Award. She has poems in *New Ohio Review, Prairie Schooner, SALT, Smartish Pace, Poetry East, Southern Poetry Review, Women in a Golden State* and others. Favorite SB food experience: Celebrating my birthday under the stars at San Ysidro Ranch, a burger topped with gorgonzola cheese and sauteed onions, and a big pile of fries.

Marsha de la O is the author of four books of poetry, *Creature* from Pitt Poetry Series is her latest from 2024. She has been awarded two book prizes—the New Issues Poetry Prize and the Isabella Gardner Book Award. She currently teaches poetry at Cal State Channel Islands.

Julie Dillemuth is a picture book author, poet, and screenwriter, with a PhD in geography. Her poetry has appeared in *Scientific American, Highlights for Children*, and literary magazines. She lives in Santa Barbara, where she can't get enough of the gluten free chocolate chip cookies from LocaVivant Kitchen. Visit *www.juliedillemuth.com* to learn more.

Alex Eleazar is a researcher, writer, and storyteller based in Goleta. Born to a British-Canadian mother and Guatemalan father, Alex was raised between upstate New York and Guatemala, eventually ending up in Santa Barbara for graduate school. Alex likes to research and write about identity, place, and community.

Mary Elliott has lived in Santa Barbara on and off for more than 30 years, always finding her way back after time in other cities. A member of the California Poetry Society, work has appeared in *California Quarterly, HAVIK*, the anthology *Crystal Fire: Poems of Joy and Wisdom*, and two Wingless Dreamer collections. She enjoys the region's simple abundance, from avocados to tri-tip cooked over an oak fire.

Kimbrough Ernest lives in Ventura with an ancient avocado tree in her backyard. She teaches poetry through California Poets in the Schools. An award winning poet, she has published in numerous anthologies, most recently *Women in a Golden State*, published by Gunpowder Press. She likes to tell a long story in a short poem.

Awe Experiencer is an enlightened folk-scriptural writer who utilizes poetry and prose to encourage friends and readers to relax and enjoy more thoroughly into their current experience. With gentle care and sincerity, he reverently writes his experiences for others to draw inspiration and beauty from. His books are available on Amazon, and other writings can be found at *AweWorldExperiencer.Substack.com*.

Judy Farris is a life-long resident of Southern California, over ten years in Santa Barbara. She loves to cook and to write and once in a while the two collide in a poem. Her favorite locally-grown food is lemons. They can be found in every category of her recipe collection, salt being the only other that comes to mind. They are beautiful and make her happy, resting in a blue bowl on the kitchen counter. It occurs to her that she has never written a poem about lemons, which will now be a persistent tickle to remedy.

Mary Freericks has an M.F.A. degree in poetry from Columbia University. She has nine books of poetry available on Amazon. The majority are memoirs beginning with *Blue Watermelon* covering her childhood in Tabriz, Iran, continuing with *Cheer for Freedom,* covering her move to Tehran and the United States. *Swimming Through the Generations* includes her five grandchildren. She also wrote *Pandemic Poetry* and *Language*. Her art is used on a number of the covers, including *From Wife to Widow*, her latest volume of poetry.

Nora Frei is a 6th grade student at Mountain View Elementary. She loves gymnastics and reading. She also loves the ocean and water. Her favorite foods are burgers, fries, and milkshakes. Poetry to her is a way to put her thoughts on paper and use her imagination in creative ways.

Kerin Friden has resided in Santa Barbara since 1980. Having grown up in New Hampshire, she was instantly besotted with our area's temperate climate and incomparable geographical setting. Not a day goes by that she doesn't feel immense gratitude for now being able to call this home! She and her late husband, Eric, owned and operated hotels, including El Encanto Hotel in Santa Barbara. Now retired, along with volunteering as a peer counselor with the Center for Successful Aging, she enjoys the challenge of creating haikus. A favorite meal enjoyed at home are steamed Hope Ranch Mussels that she has picked up that morning at Santa Barbara Fish Market and dipping freshly baked Charcoal Sesame Sourdough from Oat Bakery into the warm broth. Divine!

Mary Frink is a mother, grandmother, and the first woman Postmaster of Santa Barbara, CA. She is also a novice poet and Buddhist.

Jane Gillett is a sixth grader at Mountain View Elementary School. Jane loves reading and music, including singing, piano, and trumpet. Her favorite food is fruit. Poetry is a really fun way for her to express herself.

Danny Gonzalez is just a consciousness in a body, on a floating rock, in the ever-expanding universe, but sometimes he likes to write poetry.

Cie Gumucio is a poet, artist, and teacher. Her art installations incorporate poetry, video, and performance. She curated a TEDx event, "Rediscovery of the Senses," in Los Angeles. Cie's solo art exhibit *Writers in Search of the Sacred* explored the convergence of art, writing, and the sacred. Her poems are published in a variety of poetry anthologies. Prior to becoming a Poet/Teacher with CalPoets in the Schools, she won awards for writing in the film and television industry. A spice-infused slurp of Northern Thai Curry Noodle from Empty Bowl never fails to dazzle her senses.

Viviana Hall is a local poet, author, and literary arts advocate. Her bilingual collection *Poems of Love* earned a five-star Kirkus review and other notable critical praise. A retired mental health practitioner with a master's in social work, she brings a lifelong commitment to care and community into her work. She collaborates with various writers' organizations and produces and hosts *Poetry Now*, a local television program amplifying poetry throughout Santa Barbara County and adjacent areas.

Stephanie Barbé Hammer is a seven-time Pushcart Prize nominee in fiction, nonfiction, and poetry. Originally from Manhattan, Stephanie moved to California in 1986 to teach at the University of California, Riverside, where she taught for 30 years. Her most recent books are the magical realist mystery *Journey to Merveilleux City* (Picture Show Press), and the poetry chapbook *City Slicker: encounters with the outside* (Bamboo Dart Press). She lives in Santa Barbara with her husband, writer and political organizer Larry Behrendt.

Cece Harris is a retired medical products executive and scientist. She published her book about her work in Iran at the time of the revolution. She loves poetry and writing and is an avid reader. Santa Barbara, her beloved home since 2012, is a paradise for creativity and dreaming. She serves on the Library Board and is active in the community.

Krista Harris came to Santa Barbara at the age of 18 to attend UCSB, where she earned a B.A. in Film Studies. She's spent years telling stories about what we grow, cook, and share. As the former publisher of *Edible Santa Barbara*, she learned how deeply food connects us—to the land, to each other, to ourselves. Now she writes full-time, exploring those connections through articles, fiction, and poetry. Her favorite meals are simple and seasonal—avocados picked from a backyard tree, spiny lobster caught by a friend, wine poured as the sun slips behind the hills.

Alison Height is the owner of Los Alamos Coffee and Tea in Los Alamos, California, where she brews strong coffee, tends her garden, and writes poems inspired by community, grit, and everyday grace. Her work honors the workers, dreamers, and neighbors who bring life to small towns. When not behind the counter or scribbling lines on scraps of paper, she is raising her family, building her business, and finding poetry in the rhythm of ordinary days.

Jan Hersh is a retired children's music teacher who recently moved to Santa Barbara. She is a long standing member of the Ina Coolbrith Circle and hosted a poetry writers group in Danville, California. By day she plays piano, cello, and guitar. By night, she writes poetry. Her poems appeared in the *ICC Gathering* and *The Crazy Child Scribbler*.

Sam Hersh, a lapsed psychophysicist, lives in Santa Barbara with his muse, Jan. By day, he plays at beaches named after saints, twists porcelain, and refreshes *lactobacillus sanfranciscensis* to perfect sourdough. By night, he rewrites poetry. His poems appeared in *The Aurorean, The Ekphrastic Review, Sixfold, Monterey Poetry Review,* and *The Crazy Child Scribbler*. His favorite food in Santa Barbara is fresh catch at the harbor.

Trish Holden has been writing poetry since youth, and more intentionally since 2023 while studying with Santa Barbara Poets Laureate Perie Longo in a bi-weekly editing workshop, Laure-Anne Bosselaar in three occasional 8-week workshops, and at several workshops at the Santa Barbara Writers Conference (2024) including with Chryss Yost, Paul Willis, and David Starkey. She regularly attends the local Blue Whale series, where she has read at the open mic. Most of her poetry covers various rough and smooth fabrics of relationships, including in the context of aging. Writing about food from this perch in Santa Barbara is itself delicious.

Justin Graham Hoops is an educator and non-profit worker living in Santa Barbara, CA. He will complete an MFA in Creative Writing from Antioch University in June of 2026.

Rebecca Horrigan is an English teacher and writer. She writes for the *Santa Barbara Independent* and has been published in the *Los Angeles Times*. She enjoys practicing yoga, listening to music, and exploring nature. Her favorite SB drink is a crisp Topa Topa Kernza Lager on a Friday in the sun.

Carolyn Jabs has contributed essays and articles to dozens of publications including *The New York Times, Newsweek, Working Mother, Self, Redbook,* and *Family PC*. She is also the author of *The Heirloom Gardener*, one of the first books about heirloom vegetables, and co-author of *Cooperative Wisdom, Bringing People Together When Things Fall Apart*. Her poetry has been published by *Quartet, Brushfire, San Pedro Review, California Quarterly, Anacapa Review,* and *Evening Street Review*. She moved to Santa Barbara late in life and has the great good fortune of being a member of a poetry group led by Perie Longo.

Greg Janée can be found most mornings at Dune Coffee.

Mila Johnson is a 6th grade student at Mountain View Elementary. Mila loves playing flag football, dancing, and writing stories. Her favorite food is ramen from the Ramen Shop in Oakland, California, where she grew up. Poetry is a way to express her feelings and emotions.

Peggy Kelly is a teacher, writer, and poet, as well as a fellow of the South Coast

Writing Project, a Crystal Apple Educator Award recipient, and the author of *Peg's Picks*, a weekly email newsletter for teachers. Her writing has been published in *California English, Out of the Ground: Poems inspired by Santa Barbara Botanic Garden, Women in a Golden State, Dirigible Balloon*, and elsewhere. She looks forward each year to the first caprese salad of summer made with ripe heirloom tomatoes and basil picked fresh from the garden.

Simon Kiefer is a former urban planner who worked in New York and then Santa Barbara. In retirement, he has embraced typewriters and poetry. He offers writing workshops for anyone from teens to seniors. And he can often be found with his wife Karenina, typing impromptu poetry at the Tuesday evening farmers market in downtown Santa Barbara. The market supplies him with tomatoes he sauces for pasta he serves with chilled California Chardonnay wine—his ever favorites.

Gabriella Klein's first book of poetry, *Land Sparing*, was published by Nightboat Books as winner of the Nightboat Poetry Prize. In 2016, *Land Sparing* was nominated for the California Book Award. She received her MFA in Poetry from Vermont College and did her undergraduate studies at Wesleyan University. Gabriella is grateful for the mugwort that grows wild in her garden.

Audrey Kosek is a 6th grader at Mountain View Elementary in Goleta. Audrey loves skiing, traveling, and trying new foods. When she's not playing soccer or dancing, she likes to play with her dog, Casper. Poetry is a way for Audrey to express her feelings, like her love for tiramisu.

Lillian Kurosaka, after retiring as a writer/photographer at UCSB, became a Reiki Master and Healing Touch practitioner. Aside from her private practice, she provided these therapies at an inpatient hospice house and other facilities. She found solace in writing as a way to honor a patient's passing, and to digest being human in all ways. She is completing a book of poetry and prose on hospice patients and families she's met in the past 25 years. Her favorite restaurant is Arigato: "Their food tastes exquisite and the presentation is eye-satisfying."

Austen Lamacraft is a visiting scientist at the Kavli Institute for Theoretical Physics, UCSB. When in Santa Barbara you can find him there, in the Rec Cen pool, or in line at La Super-Rica.

Margaret Lange is a poet, writer, and songwriter from Nipomo, California. Her poems, essays, and fiction have been published in *ART/LIFE, HopeDance*, the *Tribune, Art Rag*, the *Santa Lucian*, and California Writers Club's anthologies and *Literary Review*. She is a Santa Barbara County arts commissioner representing Santa Maria, and a member of the Santa Maria Arts Council. She has worked with CalPoets, teaching poetry workshops in schools throughout Santa Barbara and San Luis Obispo Counties. Raised in Santa Maria, her family's favorite getaway was to Solvang for Danish pastry and deli sandwiches.

Elizabeth Long is grateful for the practice of writing poetry.

Perie Longo eats, breathes, and drinks poetry. Santa Barbara Poet Laureate (2007-09), author of four books of poetry and publication in significant journals. As a psychotherapist, she facilitates writing groups for bereavement at Hospice. In 2025 she received the inaugural Santa Barbara County Literary Champion Award.

Michaela McGinnis a lover of all things Santa Barbara. She considers herself a "townie" and proud of it.

Patrick McHugh established roots in Santa Barbara in the '90s after years of roaming west from Boston along the 42nd parallel. He teaches writing at UCSB and enjoys the history, the vibrant cultural scene, the food and drink, and the year-round gardening.

Amy Michelson's poetry has appeared in *Talking River, Sanskrit, The Midwest Quarterly*, Gunpowder Press and other journals and anthologies. Her poem "Mixers Speak Up" was read for the annual Spirits in the Air Event at The Good Lion in Downtown Santa Barbara. She is currently submitting her new collection, *Still Perfume*, to chapbook contests. Amy is a licensed Spiritual Practitioner at Ventura Center for Spiritual Living, and lives in Santa Barbara, California, with her husband and a dog named Boo. She is brought to her knees by a peanut butter cookie from Merci Montecito, artfully crafted from Skippy and rock salt.

Kathee Miller has been writing from her origins in New York to California, bringing an embodied connection to memory and place. A professor, poet, and photographer, she lives with her artist husband of 50 years in the foothills of SB near their son—a sommelier among other skills. Her wedding party long ago at the old Chase Bar and Grill, served up eggplant parmesan, a family favorite, and now at Ca Dario for every special occasion—stuffed artichokes. Her culinary tastes span seven decades from east to west coast. Her poetry has appeared in many books and journals.

Monica Mody is the author of the full-length poetry collections *Wild Fin* (Weavers Press, 2024) and *Bright Parallel* (Copper Coin, 2023) and the cross-genre *Kala Pani* (1913 Press, 2013). Her poems have appeared in numerous anthologies including *The Penguin Book of Modern Indian Poets* and *Future Library: Contemporary Indian Writing*, and in publications such as *Poetry International, Indian Quarterly*, and *Boston Review*. The awards her poetry has won include the Sparks Prize Fellowship (Notre Dame), the Zora Neale Hurston Award (Naropa), and the TOTO Award for Creative Writing in English.

Pilar Montes moved to Santa Barbara in 1984. Even though she lived in the LA area, a mere 90 minutes away, she had never heard of tri-tip, the unique central coast beef cut with a Santa Maria style seasoning. It became her favorite local cuisine. Three years ago, Pilar took a City College extended learning class and started writing. Pilar is director of operations for a non-profit youth orchestra program, preceded by a long career as a software engineer.

Delia Moon is a poet/memoirist who grew up in New York City and New England. She now lives in two places in California: Santa Barbara and Bodega. The earth of both places has entered her bones. She is widowed and has children, grandchildren, and great-grandchildren. She was editor and publisher of the Petaluma River Press. Her poetry has appeared in the *Bryn Mawr Alumni Bulletin* and two previous Gunpowder Press anthologies, *To Give Life a Shape* and *Big Enough for Words*.

Juliana Moore is a student, artist, and florist in Santa Barbara as well as an alumna of Westmont College. You can find her work on Instagram @artbyjulianajm and catch her playing rugby with the Santa Barbara Mermaids or arranging flowers at Hogue and Co.

Laura Mullen is a writer of poetry and hybrid works which have been published by the University of California, Futurepoem, and Otis / Seismicity, among other presses. A collaboration (*Verge*) with John David O'Brien was published in 2017, and her translation of Véronique Pittolo's *Hero* was published by Black Square Editions in 2019. Solid Objects published her ninth book, *EtC*, in 2023. Mullen's translation of Stéphanie Chaillou's first book (*quelque chose se passe*, or—in English—*something happens*) was published by Lavender Ink / Diálogos in 2025. She lives in Ventura, California.

Phoebe Mullen loves Summerland Beach Café, particularly their "Grand American Fare" French toast and hot chocolate. She lives in Santa Barbara, but received her BA in writing from Houghton College in 2021. Phoebe has published short stories in *Calliope* and *Literally Stories*. This is her first published poem.

Gale Naylor uses poetry to make sense of the world as a survivor of incest and sexual abuse. They hope their voice helps other survivors feel less alone. Gale loves the delicacies from Lilac Pâtisserie's dedicated gluten-free bakery, especially the quiche. Gale is currently pursuing an MFA at Antioch University LA, and their poems have appeared or are forthcoming in *Exposed Bone*, *Calliope-on-the-Web*, *Jupiter Review*, *The Ekphrastic Review*, and the Ventura County page of the California Poet Laureate's "Our California" website. *galejnaylor.com*

Anne Neubauer is a professional executive and local poet who resides in Santa Barbara, CA. She has been published in several anthologies, and both leads and attends national poetry workshops. Her work is inspired by spending time in nature, particularly hiking mountain trails or walking miles of California beaches.

Zilia Thien Nguyen is a writer who loves breaking bread with her loved ones, visiting gardens, and documenting everyday life using her little Sony Cybershot camera. Her favorite meal in Santa Barbara is a homemade omelet with mushrooms, over a brioche bread slightly covered in some soy sauce. She always takes her toast with a cup of tea.

Enid Osborn served as Poet Laureate of Santa Barbara in 2017-2019. She has two books in print: *When the Big Wind Comes* (Big Yes Press, 2015) and *Pedregosa St.* (Sheila-Na-Gig Editions, 2025) and she co-edited *A Bird Black as the Sun/ California Poets on Crows & Ravens* (Green Poet Press, 2011). Her poems appear mainly in West Coast journals and anthologies. Enid worked ten years for the Isla Vista Recreation & Park District as coordinator of the Community Garden Project. Before that, she worked for the IV Food Co-op. Her favorite food is baby lettuce.

Melinda Palacio served as Santa Barbara's 10th Poet Laureate. Her poetry chapbook, *Folsom Lockdown*, won Kulupi Press' Sense of Place 2009 award. She is the author of the novel *Ocotillo Dreams* (Bilingual Press 2011), for which she was awarded the Mariposa Award at the 2012 International Latino Book Awards and a 2012 PEN Oakland-Josephine Miles Award for Excellence in Literature. Her poetry collection, *How Fire Is a Story, Waiting*, was a finalist for the Milt Kessler Award, the Paterson Prize, and received First Prize in Poetry at the 2013 International Latino Book Awards. Her latest book is *Bird Forgiveness*. She also writes a bimonthly column for the *Independent*.

Tara Patrick was born in Goleta and has resided on the California Central Coast for most of her life. Her love of nature, music, and writing began early, and continues—inspired by her grandmother, mother and father, and all the various libraries she has spent time exploring in. She creates visual art from ephemera and castoffs, makes music as Diatribe Rabies Baby, and likes to climb trees.

Christine Penko was an artist-in-residence with California Poets in the Schools, teaching poetry in local schools for twenty years. She is the author of *Thunderbirds* and is also widely published in journals and anthologies. Her recent poems appear in *SALT*, and the anthology *Women in a Golden State* (Gunpowder Press, 2025). In addition to poetry, Christine writes book reviews and has completed a prose memoir. She loves the "oyster shooters" at Santa Barbara's own Brophy's restaurant and has encouraged all of her children (now adults) to try them.

Elizabeth Pérez is a Cuban American writer and associate professor at UCSB. Her favorite Santa Barbara food is sea urchin. A VONA alum, she has published poetry in journals and two edited volumes, including *El Coro: A Chorus of Latino and Latina Poetry*. In 2024, Pérez was a finalist for Wesleyan University Press's Cardinal Poetry Prize, for the manuscript *Lessons in Cuban Cosmology: Fifty-Two Poems & a Villanelle*. In 2025, she was named a finalist in Gunpowder Press's Alta California Chapbook Prize, for her submission *Refugee Lotteries*. Pérez is also the author of two award-winning scholarly books on Afro-Diasporic religions.

Kristiana Phillips is a Filipina-American poet who came to Santa Barbara to study English and philosophy and stayed for the sunsets, Western grey squirrels, and kindred spirits she's found here. Her poems have been featured in a Malaysian multi-media publication, *Romanesque*, and in Westmont College's art magazine, *The Phoenix*. When she is not wandering around Cold Springs on a quest for freckled acorns, she might be found enjoying a cup of Earl Grey with a buttered orange scone from Jeannine's.

Ariel A. Phoenix is a writer, poet, podcast host, and passionate educational rights advocate from Houston, Texas. Her work uplifts marginalized voices and sparks meaningful dialogue, rooted in a deep commitment to justice, creativity, and healing. A lover of tacos, music, and the ocean, Ariel draws inspiration from rhythm, soul, and the ever-changing tides of life. Through her words and advocacy, she invites others to rise—fierce, fearless, and free.

Peg Quinn's poetry and non-fiction have been published in numerous magazines and anthologies, four times nominated for the Pushcart Prize. Her debut poetry collection, *Mother Lode*, was published by Gunpowder Press in 2021. She lives in Santa Barbara, where she is an artist, educator, and certified beekeeper.

Diana Raab, MFA, PhD, is a poet, memoirist, poet, teacher, and author of 14 books and editor of three anthologies. Her work has been widely published and anthologized in journals such as *Rattle, Verse-Virtual, SALT, Vox Populi, New York Quarterly,* and others. Her newest memoir is *Hummingbird: Messages from My Ancestors* (Modern History Press, 2024). She co-edited *Women in A Golden State: California Poets at 60 and Beyond* with Chryss Yost (Gunpowder Press, 2025). Raab writes for *Psychology Today, The Good Men Project, Sixty and Me, Medium,* and others. Her favorite foods: fruits/vegetables and favorite drinks: tequila/soda and espresso. In that order.

Jaque Reed is a 95 year-old woman who has lived in a great many regions, North, South, East Coast and Europe, but has found a true home here in Santa Barbara. The Riviera is so aptly named that she can close her eyes, inhale the sea breezes, and feel herself back in the hills behind Nice. The oysters at Brophy's on the pier are so fresh and succulent that she cannot imagine any more luscious on the French coastline. However, the feast in her poem is purely fictional, its meaning more psychological than factual, inspired, however, by her love of feasting by the sea.

C.M. Rivers is the author of two award-winning books of poetry and works as a chef in Santa Barbara. He is grateful to be surrounded by the incredible array of food and wine on California's central coast, from Ojai to Monterey. Much to her dismay, his English bulldog is not allowed to come to work with him.

Utah Roth is a 6th grade student at Mountain View Elementary School. Utah enjoys playing water polo and Minecraft. He also enjoys hanging out with friends, family and his dog, Leia. His favorite food is a double double hamburger from In-N-Out. Poetry is fun!

Linda Saccoccio is an artist and writer. She recently exhibited her paintings at Bergamot Station in Santa Monica and has exhibited across the USA and Europe. Her poetry is published in various anthologies, journals and books, most recently *California Quarterly*. *Transitions and Translations* is a book of her paintings and the poems that accompany them. Saccoccio's ekphrastic, letterpress book collaboration is *Rigor & Sky / A Communion*. A recent favorite dish is Pane e Vino's Tagliatelle Con Funghi e Tartufo.

Eddi Oliveira Salado is a graduate of College of Creative Studies, University of California, Santa Barbara, where she majored in Creative Writing. She has been writing poetry since fourth grade. Her work has appeared in *Spectrum*, *The Los Angeles Press*, *Feminist Studies*, and many other publications. When she is not writing poetry she is riding her horse or making horse statues out of ceramics. She lives in Ventura with her husband, dogs, and horse.

Ibrahim Ibn Salma has made it his lifelong journey to discover the holiness within himself as a spiritual being. His sources are sages from various traditions, lessons found within nature, and insights from his own inner world.

Rick Sawyer is a local Santa Barbara County published author, poet, digital artist, filmmaker, beekeeper, surfer, cowboy, realtor, rancher, beachcomber, husband, and grandfather. More about his life and professional adventures can be viewed on Facebook and at *www.hollisterranch.com* and *www.ricksawyer.com*. Rick's famous saying is "Total Involvement in Functional Reality" (coined in 1968).

Charlie Schultz is an academically-talented 6th grader attending Mountain View Elementary School. With a quick wit and perpetual smile on his face, his drive to live life to the fullest could only be outshined by his passion as an athlete for all-things NBA & NFL!

Kate Schwab moved to Santa Barbara in 1995 to open Borders Books & Music on State Street. For a quarter century Kate lived on West Anapamu, a word that translates as "rising place" from the Chumash language. Fully aware that the best part of living in Santa Barbara was living right downtown, she walked to all that Downtown Santa Barbara has to offer. Kate moved to Arizona in 2020, in time to hunker down for the pandemic with her AZ family. Now retired, she spends her time with her beloved pup Millie, blogging "I'd Rather be Reading" (*k8reader. blogspot.com*), traveling, sipping Arizona wines, and searching for a creative outlet.

Jason Scrymgeour is a Santa Barbara County resident, small-business owner, and unapologetic daily drinker. After publishing poems and short stories in his twenties, he took a detour through work, life, family, and everything in between.

He's recently picked back up his habit of scribbling out words that might pass for poetry, depending on who's reading.

Jasmine Guerrero Sevilla is a Mexican-American woman who was born in Santa Barbara and raised in the Santa Ynez Valley. She is currently Santa Barbara County's Youth Poet Laureate and is studying civil engineering at Sacramento State University as a first-generation student. She has collaborated with CalNAM, co-hosted an anthology reading with Urban Word, instructed workshops, spoken before Solvang City Council, Santa Barbara Arts Commission Board, English classes at Santa Ynez Valley Union High School, and the Goleta Library. Jasmine's favorite food in Santa Barbara is from Los Agaves Restaurant.

Susan Shields was born in England during the Second World War, came to the US at 21, married an American, is now widowed. Reading and writing poetry have always been a balm for her.

Melissa Sorongon lives and works in Santa Barbara. In the summer she is always on the lookout for a good melon, and in the winter misses desperately the citrus of Mud Creek Farm.

Jacob Herrera Spears is a poet from Goleta, CA. He recently completed a B.A. in English at Westmont College after transferring from Santa Barbara City College. A poem from his senior capstone project was selected as a semifinalist in the 2025 *Rattle* Poetry Prize. His work has appeared in *Blue Unicorn* and the *Santa Barbara Literary Journal.*

Suzanne Spillman is a California native and a resident of Santa Barbara for over 50 years. She is an avid reader and collector of words and often assembles them into poems. She has been published in *AU AstroNews*, the Santa Barbara Astronomy Club newsletter, as well as *Santa Barbara Metro*. She frequently attends poetry readings, hoping to gather the courage to read some of her poems out loud.

David Starkey is founding publisher and co-editor of Gunpowder Press. He served as Santa Barbara's 2009-2011 poet laureate and is founding director of the creative writing program and emeritus professor at Santa Barbara City College. His most recent books of poetry are *You, Caravaggio*; *The Moon Shall Not Give Her Light*; and *Tell Me Why*. davidstarkey.net

Kevin Patrick Sullivan has lived in California on the central coast for fifty years. He found poetry in the wind off the ocean, the endless music of the surf, and the roar of the freeway. He was very fortunate to make many friends working in the fields of poetry. He met his wife, the artist and poet Patti Sullivan, at a poetry festival. He has a fond memory of drinking scotch with Edward Field, after dinner at Roy's after his Poetry Reading at the Contemporary Arts Forum.

Patti Sullivan's poetry books are *At the Booth Memorial Home for Unwed Mothers 1966*; *Not Fade Away*; and *For the Day*. Her poems appear in *Spillway*, *Chiron Review*, *Solo*, *Raising Lilly Ledbetter*, and several anthologies, most recently *Women in a Golden State*, Gunpowder Press. She is a life-long self-taught abstract painter and collage artist and native Californian. On moving to Santa Barbara in 1970, her first rental house was one block from McConnell's Ice Cream shop and it seemed there was a health food market on every corner. She had never experienced such cheese before!

Caitlin Swalec is a Maine blueberry at heart, living the Santa Barbara mermaid life now. Professionally, she specializes in industrial decarbonization and clean energy data. Personally, she thrives as a wild swimmer and trail runner. One of her long-term goals is to try every taqueria in Santa Barbara to find the best fish taco in town. She also enjoys exploring the world through books, writing, and nature-inspired yarn crafts.

Deborah Sykes is a 36-year resident of Guadalupe who lives in a renovated 100-year-old home. A singer, songwriter, recording artist, and graphic designer, Deborah sings the National Anthem for local veterans' groups at events and fundraisers. Although retired, she still does graphic design at no charge for non-profits and occasionally designs for local small businesses for trade.

Jennifer Moe Taylor tasted her first Blender in 1994, just ten months after Blenders in the Grass opened for business in Santa Barbara. The Red-Orange was so tasty, she invited her husband and three children to order one of their own. Blenders remains a family favorite to this day. Jennifer has lived in Santa Barbara for over 31 years. She is author of *Notes of Grace: Moments and Milestones from My Life*. "The Santa Barbara Restaurant Scene" is her first attempt at poetry that rhymes.

Daniel Thomas's third poetry collection, *River of Light*, was published by Shanti Arts in 2025. His previous books are *Leaving the Base Camp at Dawn* and *Deep Pockets*. He has published poems in many journals, including *Southern Poetry Review*, *Nimrod*, *Poetry Ireland Review*, *Amethyst Review*, *Vita Poetica*, *Atlanta Review*, and others. His favorite SB County food is his wife's gazpacho made with the tiny goodness of sungold tomatoes.

Emma Trelles is the author of *Tropicalia* (University of Notre Dame Press), winner of the Andrés Montoya Poetry Prize, and the manuscript *Courage and the Clock*, a finalist for the 2025 Donald Hall Prize for Poetry from AWP. She is the 9th Poet Laureate of Santa Barbara and has received fellowships from the Academy of American Poets, the California Arts Council, and CantoMundo. This poem was inspired in part by an outdoor visit to the Stolpman Vineyards Tasting Room in Los Olivos, with Mark & Vig—her bandmates for life.

Jace Ryan Turner is a librarian at the Santa Barbara Public Library and a poet whose work appears in recent anthologies from Gunpowder Press. A passionate walker, avid reader, and friend to many poets, he finds inspiration while soaking in the hot tub at night or in the early morning hours. Jace enjoys his plums straight from the tree—never from the icebox.

Joseph Sandy Warren retired from a 40-year career in corporate communications and now writes for the joy of it. Residing in Ventura, he makes frequent trips to Santa Barbara to visit family and enjoy the local cuisine. (The Eskimo Roll at Arigato Sushi on State Street is a personal favorite.) He frequently posts on Substack on a page titled "This and That," writing on a wide variety of subjects based on "whatever interests me at a given moment."

Leslie Andrea Westbrook is a freelance writer, community activist, filmmaker, and art dealer who loves to eat, drink and be merry. She sources her fruits and veggies at Carpinteria's Farm Cart Organics, next door to the Carpinteria Library and Friends of the Library Bookstore, another favorite haunt in her neighborhood. Half-Sicilian American, the native Californian enjoys cooking and eating Italian (roots) and Mexican food and trying out new recipes, like the Persian Love Cake she recently baked. Leslie wrote this poem in memory of a former lover and dear longtime friend, the new music composer Daniel Lentz.

Paul Willis has published eight full collections, including *Somewhere to Follow* and *Losing Streak*. His most recent gathering of poems is the chapbook *Orvieto*. He is an emeritus professor of English at Westmont College and a former Poet Laureate of Santa Barbara.

Dot Winslow holds her MFA from Antioch University Los Angeles (shout out to the Saffron cohort!) and loves food. They enjoy trying anything once, as each bite is an adventure. Their poetry has appeared in the *Santa Maria Sun* and *Waymark: Voices of the Valley* poetry magazine. Dot favors local uni and enjoys visiting Lark and Sparrow in Orcutt.

Misty Wycoff was born in Northern California to a world of high grass, crawdad creeks, and sharecropped houses close to the Pacific waters, and has resided along the bay in Los Osos for about 23 years. A retired clinical therapist and elephant seal docent, she is often found observing life on the estuaries and open waters or in her garden accompanied by her Scottish terriers Ivy and Nessa. Nominated twice for the position of Poet Laureate for San Luis Obispo County, she has eight published collections to date, including her last book, *Dwelling*, released in 2025.

Raven Wylde has been a writer of poetry, memoir, and essays since childhood. She has performed her readings at a poetry slam, in writing classes, in a telephone booth poetry recording, and in a performance for an SBCC Theater Arts event. Two of her poems appear in the 2020 *SB Literary Journal*. One poem strayed into a local library compilation. When attempting to slide a poem into a showing at a local art gallery, three paintings were displayed instead. She won a prize for best story of photographing a sex toy in public in 2019. Raven is an avocado enthusiast.

Shifra Wylder, a Boston native, studied at the New England School of Art & Design before moving to California to pursue modeling and work as a production artist in advertising. She later earned a degree in psychology and became an addictions counselor in Malibu's treatment facilities. An abstract expressionist, Shifra leads workshops that weave together art, writing, poetry, and counseling, guiding and empowering individuals toward healing. When not painting, she writes short story memoirs, poetry, and practical self-discovery guidebooks to help others deepen clarity and connection with themselves and others.

Madelyn Yee is a 6th grade student at Mountain View Elementary. Maddy loves doing football, baseball, and math. Her favorite food is sushi from Sushi Teri, or Annie's Mac and Cheese. Poetry is a fun way for Maddy to show how she feels about some of her favorite things.

Kerri Gordon Yim is a native Californian always ready for a Carpinteria beach day. She's a South Coast Writing Project Fellow, taught public school for 22 years, and volunteers with Citizens' Climate Lobby. "Wave hands like clouds" is her favorite tai chi move. Her poem "Dishes" was published in the *Postscwrip*, Fall/Winter 2023.

Chryss Yost, co-editor of Gunpowder Press, served as Santa Barbara's 5th Poet Laureate (2013-15). She received her Ph.D. in education from UCSB. A SCAD heart attack survivor, she savors every day. Her favorite forms of expression are poems and cookies.

Valerie Zell is a 6th grade student at Mountain View Elementary. Valerie loves painting with watercolor and playing with her pets. Her favorite food is beef pho and, of course, lilikoi from the island of Kauai. Poetry is expressing herself in a way that feels vibrant and free.

George Yatchisin is Santa Barbara Poet Laureate 2025-2027. He is the author of the chapbook *Feast Days* (Flutter Press, 2016) and the full-length *The First Night We Thought the World Would End* (Brandenburg Press, 2019). His poems have been published in numerous journals including *Antioch Review, Boston Review, Spillway*, and *Zocalo Public Square*. He co-edited the anthology *Big Enough for Words: Poems and vintage photographs from California's Central Coast* (Gunpowder Press, 2021) with David Starkey and Chryss Yost, and the anthology *Rare Feathers: Poems on Birds & Art* (Gunpowder Press, 2015) with Nancy Gifford and Chryss Yost.

His poetry appears in numerous anthologies including *Fantastic Imaginary Creatures: An Anthology of Contemporary Prose Poems* (Madville Publishing, 2024), *California Fire & Water: A Climate Anthology* (Story Street Press, 2020), *Reel Verse: Poems About the Movies* (Everyman's Library, 2019), and *Clash by Night: An Anthology Inspired by The Clash's London Calling* (City Lit Press, 2015).

As a journalist Yatchisin has worked for outlets like the *California Review of Books*, KCET Food Blog, *Sunset, Santa Barbara Independent*, and *Edible Santa Barbara*, and his work is compiled at his blog George Eats.

Yatchisin retired from his position as the Director of Communications for UCSB's Gevirtz Graduate School of Education in 2023.

GUNPOWDER PRESS

SHORELINE VOICES SERIES

celebrating poetic voices in our community

Women in a Golden State:
California Poets at 60 and Beyond
Edited by Diana Raab & Chryss Yost

Out of the Ground:
Poems Inspired by Santa Barbara Botanic Garden
Edited by David Starkey & Chryss Yost

While You Wait:
A Collection by Santa Barbara County Poets
Edited by Laure-Anne Bosselaar

To Give Life a Shape:
Poems Inspired by the Santa Barbara Museum of Art
Edited by David Starkey & Chryss Yost

What Breathes Us:
Santa Barbara Poets Laureate, 2005-2015
Edited by David Starkey

Rare Feathers: Poems on Birds & Art
Edited by Nancy Gifford, Chryss Yost,
& George Yatchisin

Buzz: Poets Respond to SWARM
Edited by Nancy Gifford & Chryss Yost

GUNPOWDER PRESS

CALIFORNIA POETS SERIES

In Praise of Late Wonder, poems by Lee Herrick

Gatherer's Alphabet, poems by Susan Kelly-DeWitt

Rosa Mundi, poems by Mary Ann McFadden

Speech Crush, poems by Sandra McPherson

Downtime, poems by Gary Soto

Our Music, poems by Dennis Schmitz

ALTA CALIFORNIA CHAPBOOKS

BILINGUAL EDITIONS • EMMA TRELLES, SERIES EDITOR

Alba and Other Songs, poems by Fred Arroyo

On Display, poems by Gabriel Ibarra

Sor Juana, poems by Florencia Milito

Levitations, poems by Nicholas Reiner

The First Amelia, poems by Amelia Rodriguez

Grief Logic, poems by Crystal AC Salas

COMPLETE CATALOG ONLINE AT GUNPOWDERPRESS.COM

9 781957 062303